Greg Clark
& Jimmie Frise
Outdoors

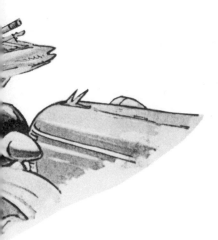

Greg Clark
& Jimmie Frise
Outdoors

Stories by
GREGORY CLARK
Pictures by
JAMES FRISE

COLLINS ● TORONTO ● 1979

Greg Clark & Jimmie Frise Outdoors
by Gregory Clark
Pictures by James Frise

This selection first published 1979
by Collins Publishers
100 Lesmill Road, Don Mills, Ontario.

©1979, the Estate of Gregory Clark and
the Estate of James Frise

The stories and pictures in this volume
were first published in the *Star Weekly*.

Canadian Cataloguing in Publication Data

Clark, Gregory, 1892-1977.

Greg Clark and Jimmie Frise Outdoors

A collection of short stories and cartoons that
appeared in the Star weekly during 1934-1940.

ISBN 0-00-216607-0

1. Natural history—Outdoor books. I. Frise,
James, 1891-1948. II. Star weekly. III. Title.

QH81.C522   500.9   C79-094656-4

Printed in Canada

The Stories

Introduction

It is in the outdoor stories that Greg Clark and Jimmie Frise come closest to reaching across the years with the humour and insight that remains as true today as when the stories were written over 40 years ago.

The first two books in this series, *The Best of Greg Clark & Jimmie Frise* and *Silver Linings* brought back the magic the author and the illustrator wove during the entire decade of the 1930's. In contrast this collection features those episodes that take Greg and Jimmie hunting, fishing, walking, skiing, boating, camping, and sailing — all things they loved to do. Their own adventures on the weekend must often have served as ready material for next week's story.

The happiness they found outdoors comes through in every one of these 24 stories. Greg and Jimmie were natural sportsmen. They preferred to be out doing things and enjoying the countryside. As these stories show, they really were the best of friends and delighted in each other's company.

Greg and Jimmie became a legend in their own time — the stories were read and loved across the country. Here, again, in these pages, you can join them once more as they head up Yonge Street north to Muskoka filled with big ideas and wonderful dreams, but destined to come up short against the reality of "almost" that seems to dog us all and make the planning before, and the telling after, the best part of the trip.

Fowl Supper

October 13, 1934

"Where are you boys from?" asked the town constable.

"This is the fourth time in a row," declared Jimmie Frise as we drove along the dreary back country road in the dusk, "that we have come home with no rabbits."

"Our wives will become suspicious," I agreed. "It looks fishy."

"We don't want any family interference in our rabbit hunting," stated Jim, "with the season just starting nicely, so I have thought up a way out of it."

"What is it?"

"We will drop into one of these farms," said Jimmie, "and each get some chickens."

"Great stuff," I applauded.

"Live chickens," said Jim. "You have that dog kennel in your yard and I have a sort of wired-off play area in mine. We will each take home half a dozen chickens, fatten them up and the local butcher will kill them for us when and as we need them."

"Jimmie," I cried, "you are a genius. You understand women. Half a dozen choice chickens, fresh from the farm, will warm their hearts more than a sackful of dead rabbits."

"You watch," said Jim, "for a sign on any of these farms we are passing that says anything about chickens for sale."

And away up there on the top end of Peel and Halton counties, over whose bleak pastures we had been pursuing the jack-rabbit in vain all day, we came down a bumpety little sideroad to a desolate-looking farmhouse, at the entrance to the lane of which our car headlights picked up the sign: "Chickens for Sale."

The farmer led us out to the chickenhouse and there we waked about fifty chickens on their perches, and the farmer, with his lantern, went along the rows of fluttering and squawking hens and selected three pair each for us at a dollar a pair.

"If you gents," he said, "will take one more pair at a dollar I'll throw a pair for nothing."

"Sold," cried Jimmie.

So the farmer spent all of ten minutes picking out the pair he would throw in.

By their legs, he carried them out to our car.

"Have you no crate?" he asked.

"No," said Jim. "I thought we would just curtain off the back of the car with my lap robe and our leather coats over the windows. They would settle down and go to sleep on the back seat all right, don't you think?"

The farmer more or less agreed and, having no pins, he got us some small nails, and we hung the lap robe across behind our front seat, and curtained the windows with the coats we rabbit hunters all carry too many of, and after each handing the farmer $4 we drove out on our way home.

11

"Good-looking fowls," said Jim, as we got back on to the bumpety road. "Nice and plump."

"That Buff Orpington I got, especially," I said. "Did you notice it? The farmer said it was under a year and a perfect roaster."

Wonderful Prospect

"Boy," said Jimmie, "we have got four or five meals of lovely roast chicken right behind us here. I like two chickens to a meal. That makes four drum sticks, four upper parts of the leg, four wings, four breasts and about five slices to a breast, making twenty slices."

"Jimmie, you make me weak with hunger."

"And those are good big chickens," went on Jimmie, intent on steering down the ragged road, "so there can be about a solid quart of dressing stuffed into them. And at this time of year apple jelly is nice with chicken. And turnips, with plenty of pepper. And the gravy! With giblets chopped up in it."

"I feel faint," I begged.

"The smell of chickens roasting," said Jim, rounding a turn and heading at last for the main highway. "We each have five pairs of chickens. That means at least five dinners, or if you are a sort of meany ten dinners in the next couple of weeks."

"I like that bit they call the oyster," I said. "You find it on the side of the bird, just under the leg."

"Don't advertise that bit," warned Jimmie. "That's a bit I always have myself, and I am terrified of my family learning about it."

"I like wings, too," I suggested.

"I like wings cold," said Jim. "Supper the day after, we will eat the two cold carcases, on which the wings have been left intact. With cold dressing, fried potatoes, you know, the smooth round kind of fried potatoes, brown on only one side."

"Aw, Jimmie, shut up!" I beseeched.

The casual clucking and fluttering behind us as the chickens adjusted themselves to their surroundings in the darkness of their curtained-off chamber had almost died away. We came to the main gravel highway that leads southeast to join the greater cement highways to Toronto. We had gone only a mile or two on it when we saw ahead the lights of a village. As we came through the village, which consists of a store, a garage and a church, we saw a crowd of cars parked around the church and its basement was gleaming with lights.

"Hooray!" yelled Jimmie suddenly.

In the night, across the front of the church entrance, was strung a banner on which was printed, to be seen dimly in the night, the words:

"Harvest Home and Fowl Supper 35¢."

"A fowl supper," roared Jimmie, slewing the car into the gravel in front of the church. "Let's go!"

"Aren't we going to get home late?" I asked.

"Listen, you've never been to a fowl supper. Come on in. Only 35 cents and all the chicken and duck you can eat. Maybe turkey. With pies and coffee and thick country bread and butter and pickles—"

We ran the car in alongside the others. Nobody was in sight, which suggested the supper was in full swing. We left the car and walked up to the steps of the church basement, where we met two ladies, who took our 35 cents each and smilingly directed us in, where a great buzz and bustle of sound and talk and an odor of good things to eat drew us like a magnet.

A Little Bit Late

The basement was jammed with men and women and ladies were waiting at the long tables set on trestles. Steaming coffee pots were passing, and a gentleman, whom we learned afterwards was one of the elders, saw us and beckoned us in and sat us down at the far end of the room amongst a group of shy young men in their Sunday clothes who were looking very red in the face and shiny and about to burst. They were eating pie in immense bites.

"We're late," whispered Jimmie as we sat down and smiled around at everybody.

"I don't want any pie," I said. "All I want is chicken and plenty of it."

13

"Duck for me," said Jimmie.

A large lady leaned over us.

"Boys," she said, "which will you have—cold ham or cold pork?"

"Chicken," said I.

"Duck," said Jimmie.

"The fowl is all gone," said the lady, beaming. "You've come late. But we have some lovely cold pork. I cooked it myself."

Jimmie and I looked around at that long table full of young men and a few young ladies, and we noticed that even the young ladies had a shiny and stretched look. They dropped their eyes when we looked accusingly about.

"At a fowl supper," said the lady with the coffee pot, "you have to be on time. I guess you boys are from the city, eh?"

"You're right," I said. "I'll have ham."

The elder who had seated us came along and helped console us. The minister worked his way down between the tables and shook hands with us and told us how sorry he was the fowl was all done, but he looked as if he had done pretty well himself.

By this time the majority had got through their pie, some of them two or three kinds, apple, mince and berry, and a few were rising and going to the exit of the basement for a breath of air and a stretch or else gathering in groups to chat about the things people chat about in church basements.

The ham came and it was a great helping, half a dozen rich cuts, the way a tired carver carves ham, half the width of the ham, thick at one edge and fading off at the other. I also had mashed potatoes, stewed corn and pickled beets. Jim had the same, only he took pork. The corn was cold, the potatoes were just warm, and I glared at Jimmie.

"Fowl supper," said I.

"We must go to one some time," said Jim, spearing a big forkful.

As we ate, the diners mostly rose and about the time the coffee pot was brought by the motherly lady, who kept passing Jim the pickles, the conserve, the bread, the butter and everything she could reach, I happened to glance over toward the door and I caught about six of the men, mostly of them youngish, standing staring coldly at us. They did not look away when surprised in this act.

"Apparently," I said to Jim, "they don't even like us to have any of their ham."

Jim looked at the door.

"Um," said he, looking away.

By unseen signals and eye glasses I noticed that everybody in the basement was gradually vanishing out the exit and through the door came the sounds of muttered excitement.

Two very large young men came in awkwardly and sat down on chairs as if guarding the door. We ate our pie and the motherly lady left us alone in the basement.

"What is this?" asked Jim.

"I don't like the look of things," I assured him.

The excitement increased and through the crowd in the exit pushed an elderly man wearing a policeman's cap. A dozen of the men and one or two thin ladies followed him. He walked over and stood across the table from us.

"Where are you boys from?" asked the town constable.

"Toronto," we said, politely enough.

"Is that your car outside, license No. L1170?"

"It is," we said.

"Where did you get the chickens you have hidden in the back of it?" asked the constable.

"We bought them," said Jimmie, a light dawning on him. "Ah, I see. You thought we were chicken thieves? Ha, ha."

"Ha, ha, ha," said I.

"You will be glad to give us the name of the party you bought them from?" asked the constable, as the ring of men and the two thin ladies gathered closer around us.

"It was a farmer," said Jim. "Let's see. It was up in the north end of the county. Let's see, we came down by . . . let's see. Look here, we have been rabbit hunting. I can't just say where we were when we bought

15

those birds."

"It was dark," I put in.

"Ah, you can't just say," said the constable softly, nodding his head. He got out a notebook and began to take notes.

"Just a minute," said Jimmie, rising to his feet. "Do you mean to insinuate that you think those chickens are stolen?"

The elder pushed forward.

"Boys," he said, "there has been a lot of chicken stealing going on in this neighborhood."

"Well, I assure you," I said, "we got them from a farmer and paid him a dollar a pair for them."

"That settles it," cried the constable. "A dollar a pair they say they paid for a lot of old hens like those."

"Several of the congregation," said the elder, "think they identify some of their own chickens. Now that Buff Orpington in there, Mrs. Sampson thinks it is her old pet hen, Chicky."

"I've had that hen seven years," cried Mrs. Sampson loudly. She was one of the thin ladies. But already the crowd was slowly and soft-footedly flowing back through the entrance into the basement and listening with averted faces to the conversation.

"This is False Arrest"

"I don't like this at all," declared Jimmie loudly. "I am a respectable citizen. I buy some hens from a farmer and . . ."

"Why had you them concealed behind rugs and coats?" asked the constable slyly, like a lawyer.

"Why did some nosey person go peeking behind those rugs and coats?" roared Jimmie.

Mrs. Sampson turned very red.

"I warn you gentlemen," said Jim, softly, tapping the table with his finger, "if I am accused by you, without any evidence whatsoever, of chicken stealing, I shall sue this municipality for ten thousand dollars. I am a respectable man. This is a false arrest."

Three of the older men, including the elder, turned

pale and hurried back to a corner, where they held a consultation.

"I warn you, too," I said loudly. "My reputation is worth ten thousand dollars. This will go hard with you taxpayers."

"Tell us where you got the chickens," demanded the constable, somewhat disturbed by the turn of events.

"You identify some of the birds," retorted Jim. "Then arrest me if you dare."

"We got the lanterns," said a man from back in the crowd.

Escorted closely by several husky young farmers, we walked through the crowd and out into the night. The crowd swarmed after us. Up to the car the constable led us. The lanterns flooded their light over the scene.

The constable carefully opened our car door.

He opened it wider.

He flung it wide.

"They're gone!" he yelled.

Our chickens were gone.

There was a moment of shocked silence.

"Who opened my car door?" demanded Jim. "Whoever opened my car door first is guilty of trespass, theft, breaking and entering! Did you open my car door, constable? If so, where's your warrant!"

"And where are my chickens?" I asked.

But in the confusion the constable and the lantern bearers and Mrs. Sampson were all swept apart from us, and in the dark Jim and I continued to shout about our stolen chickens and what we would do about it.

But nobody paid any attention. Cars were driving off with loud exhausts, lights were going on. The elder tried to engage us, but his wife drew him aside.

"Aw," said Jim, turning on his own lights.

"Anyway, it might take us a week, Jimmie," I said, "to locate that farm back in the north end of the county."

"Let's get out of this," said Jim, as if I had suggested the fowl supper.

So while Jim drove away I tore down the curtains of rugs and coats, and rearranged the rabbit guns and rubber boots.

Mighty Nimrods

November 17, 1934

I saw a gray blur as I rushed to Jimmie. "Shoot," I cried.

"It's a great pity," said Jimmie Frise, looking mournfully out the window of his studio on the roof of The Star building, "that we decided not to go deer hunting this fall."

"At our age," I comforted him, "it's a lot of trouble and a considerable expense."

"At our age," cried Jimmie. "The older we get, the less time we have left, and we should make the most of it. I'm all against young men neglecting their futures to go shooting and fishing. But after forty, every man should be encouraged to get the most out of what is left of life."

"You admit," I suggested, "that we find it a little more tiring now, tramping over the rocks and carrying out a deer?"

"The older we get," countered Jim, "the wiser we get. We are slicker at outwitting a deer, and slicker at getting other men to carry it."

"Aw, well, I'm just as glad I'm not marooned in some shanty up in the bush in this weather," I concluded.

"Old age creeping over you!" scoffed Jim. "You should be just in your prime. You should be leading expeditions of younger men into the wilds, teaching them the lore of the hunter, showing them woodcraft, instructing them in the art of shooting."

"I've reached the age," I said, "when I like to read about hunting."

"When mankind grows indifferent to the ancient arts of hunting," declared Jimmie, "mankind is getting sick."

"There certainly is something wrong with the world,"

19

I agreed. "Nobody knows what direction to look, much less what direction to go. In the past we, at least, knew what direction to look."

"This," stated Jim, "is the fag end of an age, an era. It is the exhaustion of a period in the world's history. A new age is about to be born. We just happen to be unfortunate enough to belong to the fag end. Our kids will belong to the new age. I bet they won't pass up any chances to go places and do things."

"Jimmie," I confessed, "I've got to admit something. I've got to admit that, lately, I hate even to kill a deer."

"You still enjoy roast lamb," retorted Jim. "You don't reject a nice veal cutlet, do you? And fried chicken?"

"Somehow that is different," I said.

"You bet it is different," said Jimmie. "It is different to raise a little calf from baby-hood and then cold-bloodedly knock it on the head. Think of a dear wee chickie, a little yellow fluffy baby chickie, that you raise with careful feeding, and then twist its neck all of a sudden, peel it and pop it into the oven. That's different, I agree, to going forth into the forest and hunting and killing a lordly buck in his prime."

"That's right," I admitted.

Thrill of Getting Ready

"The one way is a low, greedy, crafty, vulgar, tawdry way of living," said Jim. "The other is a man's way. If I have to keep body and soul together by carefully raising baby animals only to eat them, then I don't think there is much soul worth bothering about. But a hunter! There's a natural creature. He is worth what he can get. If he is any good, he gets a meal. If he is no good, he starves. But the way things are in civilization, even the most low, fat, unworthy, loathsome, can still breed animals and cut their throats."

"Jim," I exclaimed, "I wish we had gone hunting."

"It is too late," mourned Jim.

"Too late, nothing," I said, joining Jim at the window where he was staring out across the creeping gray city. "I read the other day there are deer within thirty miles of Toronto. Wild deer."

"Yes, but it's against the law to shoot them," said Jim.

"If there are deer that close to Toronto," I said, "you can bet your boots there are deer on the near edge of the districts you can hunt, like on the near edge of Muskoka, or in Peterboro county. We don't have to go five hundred miles for a deer hunt."

"Half the pleasure of the hunting trip," said Jim, "is going on a journey."

"We could be up to the edge of Muskoka," I pointed out, "in four hours. We could leave Toronto early in the morning and be hunting by ten a.m."

"It might be worth the try," mused Jim. "I wouldn't doubt that the boys who live in the south end of Muskoka all go farther north to hunt. There might be some real hunting in their own country."

"If there are deer within thirty miles of Toronto," I said, "there are likely to be deer within ten miles of Orillia."

And so it was arranged.

There is a thrill to getting ready for a hunting trip that in some ways is better than the trip itself. The packing of the duffle bags and packs, the laying out of scarlet shirts and mackinaw pants, the practising in throwing your rifle up to your eye in your living room.

The fingering of the rifle shells.

Early in the morning, before dawn broke, Jim was at my door, his engine throbbing, and I crept aboard in my hunting clothes, carrying my pack and rifle.

Before the town was open for business, we were through Barrie, and Orillia was just sweeping off its pavements when we sailed in and out of it. North of Orillia, we turned eastward and took a road Jim had been over years before on a fishing trip, a road that led into a country of wild swamp and bush, with only thinly scattered clearings in it and little cabins, most of them deserted for more fruitful soil.

An Exciting Runway

The sting of November was in the morning air, and as

the road grew worse and worse, the country grew more deer-like.

"Not a soul have we seen in an hour," gloated Jim. "And I just know there are deer in swamps like that one down there."

All the valleys were filled with swamps and all the hills were dense with birch and thickets, ideal for deer.

When the road became so bad that we doubted a car had been over it since September, we pulled into an abandoned clearing and prepared to scout the country for deer sign. Leaving our packs in the car, and carrying our rifles in the approved hunter fashion in the crook of our left arms, we walked up the road half a mile and then headed into a great bush that seemed to stretch for miles into the distance. Up hills and down dales, around swamps and along icy brooks we crept, searching, spying. Jim would take one side of a gully and I the other. But save for chickadees that came to inspect us and a couple of whiskey jacks that croaked in dull surprise at us, we saw no living thing.

"How about lunch?" said I. So we swung high to the left and came out on the road again and walked two miles back to the clearing and the car for lunch.

As we ate our sandwiches and drank our coffee, we planned the strategy of the afternoon.

"I like to come on a deer about four p.m.," said Jimmie. "From four until dark is the witching hour in deer hunting."

"Jim," I said, "I'm not going to carry my rifle this afternoon. I'm all of an ache. And anyway, I've got that feeling again about killing a deer."

"Those were ham sandwiches you ate," said Jim. "Isn't there something almost human about a little baby pig?"

"Stop, Jim," I said. "Anyway, I preferred the egg sandwiches."

"Can you imagine anything more ghoulish," cried Jimmie, "than eating an unborn chicken?"

"I'm going to carry my camera, Jim," I said, calmly, "and try to get pictures of a living, bounding, scaring deer, with his great flag flying. Maybe I can get a picture of you actually shooting. Wouldn't that be smart?"

22

After packing away the luncheon kit, we started out in a new direction from the clearing, a direction in which lay dark forbidding swamps of cedar and spruce. Following ridges and rocky outcroppings, we made slow progress across three or four miles of swampy and alder-thicketted country, when Jim suddenly halted and with a "whisht!" signalled me over to him.

In silence, he pointed to the mud along the edge of one of the densest of the older swamps.

"Deer!"

Deer by the dozen! Herds of deer. This was a runway such as Jim and I had never seen, it was a regular Yonge St. for all the deer of southern Muskoka. The hoof prints were fresh and some were old, as if a whole tribe of deer used it as their highway here in the lost and forsaken country.

"Ssshh!" whispered Jimmie. "I guess they travel this way to some lake ahead, for water. Let's creep along."

"Don't take the first one you see," I replied. "Wait till we come on a real big buck. Oh, boy, think of the poor guys that have gone up to the Arctic Circle for a deer hunt!"

A Defensive Shot

"Hush," said Jim, bending forward and starting the stalk. I fell in behind, unlimbering my camera and getting it open and focussed.

Along the edge of the alder swamp we followed the spoor of the deer, and across a broad flat hogback of rock, down along another swamp, where the regular pathway, filled with the little sharp pointed tracks of the deer, grew plainer and sharper as we progressed.

Jim paused to survey another wide expanse of rock ahead.

"I guess it leads to that next swamp," said he.

"Jim," I whispered, "this is one of those little pockets, those havens, overlooked by covetous men, where a community of deer has survived as in the pioneer days."

"Hush," said Jim, bending low again and leading on.

Past the rock and past the next swamp we bent,

watching with the eagle eye of the trained deer hunter for the slightest movement, the slightest gray shadow that would indicate a buck moving in the tangle.

As we came around the end of the swamp, there suddenly spread before us a low hill on which was a clearing and in the near side of the clearing was a fence.

And at a gate in the fence, timidly bunched together as if waiting for an expected arrival to open the gate, stood a flock of about thirty Muskoka sheep!

"Heck!" said Jim.

"Ha, ha," said I, "the joke's on you! Sheep!"

"Watch out!" said Jim, quietly.

"Just a second," said I, stepping out to one side, "till I take your picture. Hold your rifle up as if you were shooting."

"Watch out!" yelled Jim, sharply.

Out of the corner of my eye, I saw one of the sheep had detached itself from the dense packed flock, and on mincing feet was dancing toward me.

"Ram!" yelled Jim. "Jump!"

I saw a gray blur as I rushed to Jimmie. "Shoot!" I cried. "Jimmie."

"Bang!" went Jim's rifle, pointed in the air.

The ram curved away and on dancing feet, he circled back towards his flock, shaking and lowering his head.

"Jim," said I, "let's get away from here."

"Don't get tangled in my feet," protested Jim. "Why didn't you bring your own rifle?"

The ram was coming again, head shaking and feet dancing. And then over the hill came a man running. He was one of those leaden, leathery Muskoka farmers.

"Hayah!" he rasped at the ram, and the ram curved away, while the farmer opened the gate and let the frightened flock go scampering through into the pasture beyond. The ram followed them.

"So," said the farmer. "Sheep shooters, huh?"

"I beg your pardon," said Jim and I.

"So You're the Guys"

"So," said the farmer, eyeing us cleverly, "you're the guys been shooting up my flock?"

"We just fired to scare the ram," I stated. "We fired in the air."

"Then how is it," asked the farmer, grimly, "one of my sheep is dead?"

"Where is it dead?" we asked indignantly.

"Follow me," said the farmer, wheeling. He led us through the gate and across a hundred yards of pasture to a large stone. And in the bushes at the bottom of the large stone, lay a dead sheep.

"There," said he.

"But," protested Jimmie, for we could smell the sheep, "that sheep has been dead two or three weeks!"

"You fired a shot," said the farmer. "The sheep is dead. That will cost you four dollars."

"But where is the bullet hole?" I asked brightly.

"On the under side," said the farmer. "Turn it over and see for yourself."

"You turn it over," said Jim.

"No, you turn it over," said the farmer. "It's you that doubts there is a bullet hole in it."

"Listen, this is preposterous," cried Jimmie.

"You fired a shot, didn't you?" demanded the Muskoka farmer, thinly.

"Yes, but . . ."

"Very well," said the farmer, logically, "I let you have it at four dollars, a bargain price, in view of the fact the sheep isn't strictly fresh."

"Suppose we don't pay, what will you do?" asked Jim.

"I'll follow you out to wherever your car is parked," said the farmer, "and I'll take your number, and I'll swear out a warrant against you."

Jim and I looked at each other. Then we both dug down for two dollars. After all, the shot had been fired in my behalf, to halt a charging ram.

The farmer took the money.

"Good day," said we shortly.

"What I can't understand," called the farmer after us, as he watched us depart, "is how a fellow can get any sport out of shooting a sheep!"

But Jimmie and I just kept walking straight on.

Ski
High
February 9, 1935

Before I could gather my wits, I was shooting into space, and in a blur beneath I saw a lot of brown sand, trucks and a steam-shovel.

"Sooner," said Jimmie Frise, "or later you are going to ski."

"That is one of the pastimes of this raddled era," I countered, "which I will give a bye."

"A little bunty guy like you," went on Jimmie, "should love skiing. Now you take a long lanky fellow like me. When I fall, I fall plenty. By the time I have fallen my full length, I have gained enough whip-like momentum to cause my head to snap like a pistol shot."

"Little men fall as hard as big ones," I assured him. "It is all relative. The parts on which I fall hurt just as much as yours."

"Skiing is a grand sport," begged Jim. "A grand, modern sport. A sport on a par with the tempo at which we live. It is fast, smooth, exciting. It is as swift as aeroplaning. It is as smooth as motor racing. It is as bracing as modern music. It is streamlined sport."

"For streamlined people," I reminded him. "I have lost my streamlines."

"That is nonsense," argued Jim. "You are just hedging. You can have no idea what pleasure you are missing. I would say, to look at you, that you would be a really first-class skier. Maybe a great skier. You have a sort of Norwegian look."

"My ancestors," I protested haughtily, "were Scottish shepherds."

"Ah," cried Jimmie, "all the more reason you should ski. Your Scottish blood should cry out for the hills, the bracing heights, the thrill of diving, as your ancestors must have dived down out of the highlands into the lowlands. I bet if the Scottish clans had had skis, the English would never have conquered them."

"The English never did conquer them," I shouted.

"You accepted our king," protested Jim.

"We did nothing of the kind," I repeated in a loud Scottish tone. "After the failure of our plans for Prince Charles, we accepted a German king. No English king would be accepted by any Scot. No, sir!"

"But you admit your Scottish blood ought to respond to the thrill of skis," pleaded Jimmie. "You will admit that it should have been the Scots, and not the Norwegians, who thought of skis."

"I admit that," I agreed. "And I must say, if we had

skis in Scotland in the time of Montrose or Prince Charles, for example, the history of the world would be far different."

"You should, for patriotism's sake, try skiing," said Jim.

"I might," I grudged.

"Furthermore," mused Jim, gazing out of his studio window across the shining city to the far white hills to the north, "it takes you out into the company of the young. It is bracing. Inspiring. These brave young people of today. Brave and gallant.

"I'd go almost any time," I admitted.

"Good," cried Jimmie. "Have you got an outfit?"

"I can borrow my young brother's skis," I said.

How Gay and Free!

So we waited for the right kind of a day. It is a curious thing that while we in Toronto slather and slabber around in slush, with nary a patch of white snow anywhere in the city, just a few miles north, above Richmond Hill, the snow begins, and inside of an ordinary golf club run of the city, you are amidst the loveliest of snows. And of hills. It is a fact nobody but the market gardeners knew until the ski clubs brought the fact to Toronto's attention.

Three big carloads of us went north of the city for the afternoon. Only a little way outside the city limits, we joined a procession of cars, most of which had skis projecting.

A little way past the jail farm, we began to see figures out on the fields, skiing.

"I wish it were a little more graceful on the flat," I suggested to Jim. "Sliding down a slope, they look beautiful, birdlike. But on the level, they have a curious waddling appearance. I can't say I care much for the sight of baggy-clothed people waddling, however bright their cheeks or starlike their eyes."

"They call it ski-running, on the level," said Jim.

"Ski-waddling, it should be," I said.

As we went farther north, the fields became hillier and more studded with skiers. Some of them were sliding.

They slid down in four seconds and then took ten minutes to waddle back up again.

Now and again, you would see somebody more skilful than the rest who, with the help of his ski poles, would go half-running and half-sliding across the level fields, in a most airy fashion.

"If they had some sort of a gadget for re-climbing the hills," I remarked.

"They have," assured Jim. "They have strips of seal skin with the hair pointing backwards. It is smooth and skiddy forward, and takes hold with a backward push."

We came to greater hills and turned out to the left on a country road which led to a series of rolling hills and, alongside the roadside, many cars were parked.

"Here we are," cried Jim.

And our cavalcade joined the show. Out of the cars tumbled the strong young people, and immediately started buckling on their skis. They removed their heavy coats and stood forth in light and silky blue coats with flat-topped caps and strong trousers.

"How gay and free they look," I cried to Jim. "What had their mothers to compare with skiing? Just going to the rink and circling round and round on their beau's arm, to the music of a band. I recall the tunes, 'Ask Her While the Band Is Playing?' "

"Their grandmothers," said Jim, as he bent to snap the rugged buckles of his ski harness, "were worse off. The best they could do was get in a cutter and go for a drive. Their fussy clothes buried under heavy buffalo robes. Their little faces, framed in bonnets, peering timidly above."

"I wonder," I sighed, "where all the feminine types have vanished?"

For over the fences and away raced the young people, the girls as strongly and stridingly as the boys, with never a tumble and never a scream or a squeak. In fact, a good many of the girls had baritone voices.

And Jimmie and I followed.

A Beginner's Hill

Skis have no sense of direction. They are not like

29

boots. You can trust a boot. But you can't trust a ski. If it doesn't turn in, it turns out. It never wants to go straight. The first thing you do is have the right one cross over the toe of the left and you go down on your arms, pushing snow up your wristbands. The next thing you do is spread them out at forty-five degrees, in which event the only thing you can do is sit down.

If you lean backward as you slide down a little grade, you sit down. If you lean forward, you sit down anyway. The first lesson in skiing is sitting down.

But so jolly is the atmosphere of skiing, that you pretend you like the business. And by the time you reach the top of the hill where the others are gathered, you are so angry that you laugh.

Jim had preceded me up the hill. It wasn't a very big hill. In fact, in summer it would only be a little slope on which cows would stand chewing. And even in winter, if you had enough sense to walk in your boots, it would not be a hill so much as a bulge. Jim spread his skis out pointing in opposite directions and waddled up. I followed. They call it herring-boning. It is very hard on leg bones, too.

At the top of the hill, I discovered the view. For on the far side of the hill was a terrific slope down to a far-distant stream bed. Down this half-mile slope, skiers were swooping and skidding in clouds of white. Fast down they went, and slow up they came, in groups and parties and singles. Their bright cries rang across the far wide white.

"Mercy," I said.

"This is really only a beginners' hill," said Jim. "Watch the kids go down."

They were departing in singles and doubles. Down the wide slope they raced, with gathering speed.

"Be careful to the left," said Jim. "That's a sand pit. There is a road for trucks there. You can't see it from here."

"I've no intention of going that way or any other way," I assured Jim. "I am here to observe. I always observe, first."

"Oh, come on," urged Jim. "It's as simple as can be.

Just stand up and let her rip."

"I'll observe." I repeated, preparing to sit down in case Jim gave me a shove.

"Well, here goes," said he.

And with a couple of shoves with his ski poles, and bending to meet the breeze, Jim launched himself off the hilltop and sped, growing smaller and smaller, into the distance, curving past other skiers, a trim eagle of a shape, soaring across the white expanse.

Half a dozen girls and men were on the hilltop and as they launched themselves away, others arrived. I stood in the bright winter afternoon, watching them, admiring them. They were so healthy and gay. They flung themselves off the hilltop so carelessly, to go swooping a mile a minute into the far valley.

Presently, I saw some of Jimmie's party toiling up the sides of the slope, and at last came Jim himself, his long legs working like scissors as he straddled his way, herring-boning, up the snowy hill.

By the time Jim got back to the hilltop, there were about twenty of us there, and I drew aside so that if Jim wanted to do any more coaxing or urging of me, he would not be doing it in front of these nice young folk.

"You saw me?" asked Jim. "Well, what's hard about that? You just stand up."

"Let it go, let it go," I said. "Don't keep at me in front of all these kids. They'll think I am scared."

"Well, what are you?" asked Jim.

"I'm just cautious," I said. "I like to look before I leap."

Two or three of the bright girls came over and joined us. I backed up to give them room with their skis.

I backed up by giving myself a little shove with my poles. I felt myself moving mysteriously away from them. I looked at them in astonishment and saw a look of horror on their faces. Especially Jimmie's.

"Whoa," yelled Jim.

I felt myself moving a little faster and I knelt forward. I reached out to clasp the earth. I felt myself tangle and roll up. I heard a clatter of my skis. Then I found myself headed forward and I stood up.

It was beautiful.

I stood up carefully and concentrating on the toes of my skis, away out ahead of me, I raised my arms from my side and let her rip.

As I zoomed, I noticed I was not in danger of colliding with any other skiers, either going down or coming up. They were away off to my right.

Suddenly I remembered Jimmie warning me against the sand pit. I peered ahead squinting my eyes against the icy wind. My heart stopped. But I stood rigid. Because I could do nothing else.

Far behind me I heard faint yells and screams.

But before I had time to decide what to do, if anything, I felt myself shoot into a spin and all in a blur, I beheld right under me a lot of brown sand and a truck moving and some little shanties and a steam shovel.

It was only six feet from where I went over the side of the pit on to the top of the pile of sand in the moving truck.

I landed in a sitting position, on the freshly shovelled and slightly warm sand.

The truck, in low gear, ground its way out of the sandpit and turned up the road. I shouted. I rattled my feet so that the skis tapped the cab of the truck. But the noise it was making covered up the sounds. Shifting my seat on the sand, I stuck one ski out beside the little rear view mirror that projected from beside the driver. I waved the ski tow in front of the mirror.

Giving Them a Thrill

The truck stopped.

The driver hung out of the cab.

"What the . . ." he said.

"I happened," I explained, "to fall into your truck from the top of the sandpit."

"Will I help you down?" he asked.

"If you don't mind," I said, "drive me to the road to where those cars are parked and let me off there. It will save me climbing back up the hill."

He disappeared back in the cab and in thirty seconds,

we were up beside the parked cars. The driver got down and assisted me to alight. I thanked him and proceeded to climb the little slope we had gone up when we first arrived.

When I reached the top, there wasn't a soul on the hill. But down to the left over by the sandpit where I had made my leap, there were fifty people all gathered, in a dense dark mob, while figures slid and dodged about.

"Halloo!" I shouted.

The crowd stared up.

"Halloo, Jimmie," I bayed, waving my ski poles.

Up that hill they came dozens of them. They came waddling and herring-boned and some of them took off their skis and came legging it.

Jim was in the lead.

"Holy herring," he bellowed, when he got near me, "we've been looking all over that pit for your corpse!"

"I'm no corpse," I called.

"But we saw you," gasped Jim, as he made the grade, "we saw you, with our own eyes, go over that pit!"

"Sure you did," I said, and lighted a cigarette like in the rotogravure. The crowd massed around me, staring with interest and astonishment.

"But, but," spluttered Jimmie, "how did you get back up here so quickly?"

"Pshaw," I murmured, "I didn't know you were looking for me. I saw you all rushing down there while I was herring-boning back up here."

Jim just stared. And all the young girls stared, too, sort of sideways—you know the way. One of them asked me if I was going to do it again.

"I don't care for these little hills, I explained to her and the others, quite pleasantly. "After Switzerland, you know? But go ahead, I'm here to watch the fun. Go ahead."

And I rested on my ski poles, watching the others sliding and chatting from time to time with little groups who gathered round. Because as the afternoon wore on, I thought up more and more of my strange and exciting adventures in skiing all over the world.

In fact, everywhere but Toronto.

Camping

July 20, 1935

"The editor," said Jimmie Frise, "is off for a few days buying paintings for the picture section."

"Then," I said, "let's go fishing."

"Not fishing," said Jimmie. "I am tired of fishing. Let's go camping. There is a sort of anxiety and hurry about going fishing. Camping, you can just dope along."

"Morally," I hesitated, "we are justified in sneaking off like this when the editor goes away. Because it is far, far better that we should take care of our health than that we should just stick to the mere letter of the law. We aren't Pharisees, I hope."

"Both for the sake of our employers," said Jim, "as well as for the sake of our families and dependants we should use our initiative in the matter of keeping well and efficient. How long do you suppose the editor will be away?"

"Let's take a chance on four days," I estimated.

"I feel poorly," admitted Jim. "I really do. I feel the need of a few days drowsing in the shade beside some cool lake. The editor doesn't go away now as much as he used to, does he?"

*Rusty thrust his head in the tent,
a black and white object in his
jaws . . .*

"We don't get quite as much opportunity for using our initiative in the matter of our health and well-being," I confessed. "Let's take a chance on three days. Nobody will notice it."

"You remember the time he came back in two days?" warned Jimmie.

"We must remember," I said, "not to get sunburned. When a boss comes back and finds his whole staff all sunburned it gives rise to suspicions. We working-class people are pretty dumb. You notice the assistant bosses always go golfing on dull afternoons?"

"By jove," admitted Jim.

"With our families all away," I proposed, "we can just go on a nice little camping trip, the kind all men want to take but never can. Most men are prisoners. They can't do what they like at the office. And they can't do what they like at home. And when the so-called holidays come the poor fellow has to go where the family tell him. Now's our chance for a three-day escape from prison. Where will we go? Peterborough? Parry Sound?"

"Suppose," said Jim, "suppose we just get in the car, with a tent and some pots and pans and some grub, and turn either left or right at every fourth gallon of gas?"

"A perfect idea," I cried. "You drive and I'll watch the gas. And at every fourth gallon we'll take the next turn."

"Real gipsies," exulted Jimmie "Wotting not whither we goeth."

"We won't fish. We won't even hunt birds' nests. We'll just dangle along all day and when five o'clock comes we'll look for a place to pitch our tent and there we'll pitch it."

"And," sang Jimmie, "if we don't feel like getting up in the morning we won't. And if we find a nice shady spot by a cool lake, we'll just stay there. We don't have to keep on going, do we?"

"Not at all," I agreed. The only rule will be, however, that at every fourth gallon we take the first turn, either to the right or the left, it doesn't matter."

"Swell," said Jim.

To The Wide Open Spaces

So, after making a few discreet inquiries around the editor's secretary and trying to find out from the art department how many paintings it needed for the next while, Jimmie and I quietly slipped away and went to our homes and packed.

"Don't take much," ruled Jim. "Your little tent, and my outboard motor . . ."

"We're not going fishing," I cut in.

"It will be handy to have along, in case we want to go for a spin somewhere."

"And my gasoline stove," I added.

"And Rusty," submitted Jim.

Rusty, his Irish water spaniel, had been left home by the family because it takes him so long to get acquainted with the other dogs up at the cottage. In fact, it takes the whole two months, July and August, for Rusty to get on speaking terms with the dogs of the beach.

"Very well, bring Rusty," I conceded. "You can't very well leave him for three days."

And soon Jimmie and I were, with a carefully filled and measured gas tank, on our way up Yonge St. for the wide open spaces.

It was a beautiful day. We who rarely see the highways except when they are frantic with weekend traffic can have no real appreciation of this beautiful land of ours as it appears when leisure fills the main roads and the lush fields wave and blow in the summer wind.

"Ah, Jimmie," I said, "to think of all those poor chaps and poor girls back in town, sweltering over desks, dancing attendance on machines, tools, boxes, bales. Couldn't life be wonderful if only we knew how to arrange it?"

"Canada," said Jim, waving one arm off the steering wheel, "Canada, my own!"

The lazy miles whipped by.

"Curious," said Jim, "that we put on speed every time we hit a good pavement and so the sooner get off it on to a bad one. Why don't we go slow over a good highway and fast over a bad one?"

"It would be more sensible," I confessed.

So we cut down to twenty-five miles an hour and felt Yonge St., beyond Aurora, peel off under us yard by yard at a lovely sightseeing pace.

It was between Barrie and Orillia that the four-gallon mark arrived, at which we had to turn either right or left. So we turned right, across a country road that led us down to Lake Simcoe.

"This means," said Jim, "that we should follow around the lake and cross into the Kawartha district."

"So be it," I agreed.

And through Atherley we drove, following the highway southward and looking, since evening was drawing on, for a handsome place to pitch our gipsy tent.

"Clouding up," commented Jim.

And out of the west, large majestic white clouds were rearing themselves vastly, with might, gleaming edges and dark shadows in their midst.

"Did you get the tent repaired that place?" Jim asked.

"I can put a towel over it," I said. "It isn't much of a hole."

"Let's turn left over towards Bobcaygeon," said Jim.

"Not till four gallons are gone," I pointed out.

But we'll be back in Whitby before another four gallons," protested Jim.

"We'll find a good spot along here soon," I said, looking out at the clouds. "What I like about Ontario is the infinite variety. All kinds of earth, rock and soil. All different trees, hardwood here, spruce there. And all kinds of weather. There is no sameness about this country. If it had stayed bright and blue all day, like it was this afternoon, we'd soon weary of it."

"I like a storm," agreed Jim, also looking over his shoulder. "There is something bracing about it."

And Rusty, sleeping on the dunnage bags in back, got up and yawned and looked out, too. He whined.

"There's a spot," exclaimed Jim.

We were north of Brechin somewhere, and off to the left, sweet rolling meadows, sloped with spruce and cedar and topped with clusters of birch and pine, beckoned us.

Without conversation, Jim took a rutty little side road. In five minutes we were stopped at the foot of as perfect a camping spot as ever gipsies found. A small bright brook went by the sloping meadow. Birches on a flat-topped hillock stood ready to shelter our little tent. Grass and herbage made a ready couch for our blankets.

"My own Canadian home," lilted Jim.

And a faint mutter of thunder applauded him.

"Here," I said, "let's get the tent up right away."

So while Rusty went exploring, Jim and I cheerfully unloaded the car and carried the little silk tent up the slope. Picked a level spot for it to pitch. Strung the rope between two graceful birches. And in five minutes, our home was ready.

"Let 'er rain," laughed Jimmie.

And we looked at the towering clouds, which now were much higher and higher, and from them hung down ragged smoke-colored remnants, sweeping towards us.

"Let's get the stuff in the tent," I cried.

Blankets and corrugated box of grub, gasoline stove and pots and pans.

"I'll just bring this outboard motor in," said Jimmie.

"Leave it," I hurried, two big drops starting to swing down at us. "There isn't room in the tent."

"Car doesn't lock," shouted Jimmie, for a gale suddenly bent everything over. "Sure to be stolen if I leave it in the car."

So he staggered the engine up and we just shoved into the tent as the first deluge plunged down out of the clouds.

"Here, Rusty, Rusty, whit, whit," whistled Jimmie, Rusty having disappeared.

"Shut the flaps," I shouted.

The little tent was all cluttered and abulge with bundles, boxes, stove, engine, pots and what not. I sat on the stove and Jim on the tank of his engine.

And the little tent bellied and flapped loudly with the gale, while a regular thunder of rain beat, like bursting ocean waves, against the frail silk.

These summer showers," I cried, "are soon over."

Troubles Multiply

"Thank goodness," called back Jimmie, "we have your little gasoline stove. Dry wood won't be found after this."

"We forgot to get gas for it," I remembered. "We can siphon some out of your car tank."

"If we have a siphon," shouted Jim.

And then thunder roared and lightning hissed and cracked, and Jim found a small stream starting to run under the tent and across the ground.

"Get off the stove," said Jim, "and I'll set the grub box on it to keep it dry."

"So I stand up?" I inquired.

I half stood up and half sat down, while the walls of the tent sagged looser and looser, and the thunder growled and the ground grew all wet, and we kept shifting things around in the cramped tent.

"I wish I knew where Rusty is," said Jim.

"Fighting some local dog," I suggested.

"Rusty hates rain," said Jim.

"Sure, he's a water spaniel," I explained.

Jim peeped out the tent flaps.

"Very black over by the east," he said.

"Sometimes, these summer storms that come up in the late afternoon," I said, "mean an all-night rain. And a westerly blow."

"Rusty, Rusty, whit, whit," went Jim out the tent flaps.

"Aw, let him alone," I exclaimed. "He's probably found somebody his own size."

The rain seemed to slacken.

"Jim," I said, "while I'm seeing if there is any gas in this stove tank, take a run down to the brook and get a pail of water so we can make tea. It looks like an indoor supper tonight."

When Jim was gone with the pail, I looked, and as I fully expected, there was no gas in the stove tank.

Jim scratched hastily in through the flaps.

"The creek," he said, wiping rain off his face, "is running yellow mud. Pure mud."

So we sat and listened to the thunder and blinked to the lighting and shoved articles of furniture up against the corners of the tent to keep the steadily sagging walls from coming entirely in upon us.

Ants, spiders, striped worms and small beetles began climbing up everything that was dry, such as us.

"Pshaw," said Jim, "think of our poor ancestors who came to this country in the early days. They didn't even have tents. They had to rush up some kind of a roof over their heads, made of split logs. Think of being huddled in here with all your family, including little babies, in a storm like this. And they had storms like this in 1800."

"Our ancestors," I taught Jim, "were simpler folk than we. They came from mud huts in Ireland and shacks made of granite rocks in the Highlands. My ancestors used to have the chickens roost on the foot of the bed when they first came to Ontario."

"What I mean," said Jim, pulling his feet up under him," is that we ought to have just underneath our skins, the makings of good men. Tough men. Men who can suffer hardship like this. It can't have gone out of us completely in only two or three generations."

"I wish I had my plus-fours on," I said. "Did you ever have any ant up your pant leg? I don't think our ancestors wore pants."

"Think," said Jimmie, brushing off a couple of spiders and a small green hump worm, "of our Scottish ancestors, coming in to this country in kilts."

But a loud flash and bank of lightning made us stop thinking of our ancestors. The ground was now swishy under our feet. The rent in the tent that we had got last fall was dripping water into the left rear corner, and I was in the right.

"Skunk," said Jim suddenly.

"Phew," said I.

And Rusty thrust his dripping wet face in the flaps.

"Get out," I yelled.

Rusty backed out. But in a moment he thrust his head in again, this time gripping in his wide jaws, and his eyes gleaming proudly above, a black and white object limp in his jaws. And of overpowering fragrance.

"Get out. Scat."

Even Jimmie threw a pail at him.

Hating To Admit Defeat

And so we had whines from Rusty outside, to add to the things we had to listen to, as the darkness continued to deepen, and the thunder went away and then came suddenly and surprisingly back again. And the wind changed direction and began shoving at the front flaps.

"Jim," I said, "we can't stay here."

"Let's wait and see," said Jim.

"Put that engine out and give us some room," I insisted.

"Nothing doing," replied Jim.

"We have no water, no wood, no gas for the stove," I complained.

"Maybe it will clear," said Jim.

"That dog," I said, "has put the kibosh on everything. I can hardly breathe."

"We have to take him home in the car," pointed out Jim.

"I say we beat it," I concluded.

"Where to?" asked Jim.

One hates to admit defeat. I gazed hopelessly about the little tent, its dripping walls sagging close to our heads.

"Jimmie," I cried, looking about at the grass and herbage on which our beds were to be laid. "What's that plant right beside you there!"

"Gee," said Jim, drawing up his hand.

It was three-leaved, glossy green, with reddish tinges at the base of the leaves. It was cool, cold, cruel looking.

"Poison ivy, Jim," I gasped.

"I guess we had better go," agreed Jim half rising, which was all he could do.

And as we stepped out the door, a long glorious blade of evening sunlight burst across the glade. The dripping world shone and sparkled. Rusty barked hoarsely and started to show us his latest victim.

"How about it?" asked Jim. "We'll go. But where?"

"Home," I said, for both of us.

And into the back of the car we stuffed the soaking tent, just bundled in anyhow, and the engine and the stove and the grub box. Jim scrubbed Rusty with bunches of grass, to no purpose.

"Zing," said something.

"Now the mosquitoes." said I.

And before we had the car loaded the soft, muggy summer evening was alive with great big after-the-storm mosquitoes, focussing on our ankles and wrists.

"Make it snappy," said Jim.

"I'm ready," I snorted. "What about Rusty?"

"Whit, whit," said Jim to Rusty, and Rusty, all damp clambered in.

And under a radiant starry sky, we drove down to Whitby.

"Four gallons, exactly," said I, as we rounded the turn to Toronto."

And so to bed.

Bear With Us

August 3, 1935

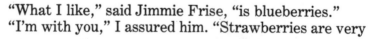

"What I like," said Jimmie Frise, "is blueberries."

"I'm with you," I assured him. "Strawberries are very

With his front feet held quaintly before him, the bear surveyed me across the bushes . . .

nice, if they aren't sandy. But they give me hives. Rasp-
berries are good, if they haven't got little white bugs
creeping about them. And raspberry seeds get between
my teeth."

"Thimbleberries," contributed Jim, "aren't bad, but it
is hard to get a feed of them. I like a feed of wild berries."

"The wild strawberry," I took on, "is probably the finest wild berry in the world. The French-Canadians preserve them."

"Yes, but give me blueberries," said Jimmie. "I don't
mean blueberries you get in the city, with the blue down
all rubbed off them, and looking kind of damp. I mean
blueberries you pick yourself and eat right out on the
rocks."

"I follow you," I assured him.

"They are so tight, in their skins," said Jim. "They
burst, they pop in your mouth."

"Like celery, sort of," I helped.

"Not at all," said Jim. "Nothing like it. They are alone,
unique, unequalled. Tight in their skins, with that cool,
downy powder on them, and a kind of faint wild spicy fla-
vor."

"That's it," I moaned. "Faintly spicy."

"Not rough and harsh, like Oriental spices, but a deli-
cate Canadian spiciness," said Jim. "Dear me, excuse
me, my mouth is watering."

He got out his handkerchief and attended to himself.

"The thing I like about them, too," went on Jimmie, "is
the way they burst in your mouth, a whole big handful of
them."

"Do you like the bright blue ones or the darkish, black-
ish huckleberry kind?" I inquired.

"Well, it's hard to choose," agreed Jim. "The dark ones
often have a rich spiciness, yet on the other hand, the
bright blue ones have a kind of tang. I don't know."

"The bright blue ones," I pointed out, "are lovely to
come on when you are wandering around on the rocks,
blueberry picking. You walk along, looking here and
there, and then all of a sudden, in one of those big cracks
or crevices in the rocks, you see a whole hedge of little

bushes that are a vivid sky blue."

"The Jesuit Relations say," stated Jim, "that in the olden days, away back in 1600 and something, the Indians used to pick great bushels of blueberries and spread them out on the rocks to dry and then pack them in big birch bark sacks. In the winter, they would use these dried berries to eke out their dog meat and pounded corn porridge."

"I prefer to think of going somewhere this afternoon," I submitted, "and picking about two quarts of blueberries and eating them right there as I pick. I'm blueberry conscious."

"There's no place handy where we can go on short notice," Jim thought. "Wonder if there are any blueberries this side of Muskoka or Parry Sound?"

"Would you be game," I inquired, "to take a run up as far as Midland and hire a boat and go out to one of those rocky islands that are fairly covered with blueberries?"

Doing Something Silly

"Do you mean in the middle of the week?" Jim exclaimed. "That would be silly."

"Everybody ought to do something silly once in a while," I offered, "like loosening those little twisters on the end of a banjo handle, so as to relax the light wires. We're full of tight wires. Can you think of any silly thing to do that would be as pleasant as driving up to Midland and hiring a little boat and going somewhere to bulge ourselves with blueberries?"

"This heat is getting you," suggested Jimmie.

"I'm full of tight wires," I said. "I'm going to reach up and loosen those little tighteners. I'm going to do something silly. And it might as well be pleasant."

"I could go," said Jim, "and think. Us artists have to do some conceiving. We ought to be free to run off and hide now and then to invite our souls."

"The same with writers," I agreed. "You can't make a flower grow by walking out every day and yelling, 'Grow, damn you, grow!, can you?'"

"Artists and writers," said Jimmie, "are just like flowers. The heat gets them."

"How about it?" I demanded.

"How long would it take?" asked Jim.

"If we drove tonight," I said, "we'd be there in three easy hours. Sleep in the car, right in the tourist camp. Rise with the lark, drive down and hire a little launch for a couple of bucks, and scoot half an hour out across the lovely morning water . . ."

"That's done it," said Jim.

"Spend from, say, seven or eight o'clock till noon picking and eating berries," I said. "Then the boat picks us up by prearrangement and scoots us back across the lovely water to Midland, we hop in the car, and saturated with that noble and patriotic berry, we drive home to Toronto, arriving about 3 p.m., much to everybody's astonishment."

"What would we say?" asked Jim.

"We'd say we slept in, or something," I offered. "Or maybe in this heat nobody would have observed our absence,"

"Well, I guess," said Jim sleepily.

And before the five o'clock whistles had stopped blowing in the suburbs, we were pointed north for Midland. And the sun was still high when we arrived in that pleasant town. Under the long, lingering sunset, we watched the boats coming and going, probably driving their launches fifty miles for a package of phonograph needles or a camera film. So busy. So intent.

And with the floating sounds of summer in our ears, we folded ourselves up in Jim's big car and went to sleep. Dawn and a cramp woke us. We took no breakfast, though the light was still burning in the Chinese restaurant as we drove down the street to the docks. The man we had hired the night before was sleepily waiting for us in his little putt-putt. It was just a row-boat with an engine in it, but it could not have been better.

Gaily Across the "Open"

"If it is blueberries you want," said the boatman, steering out into the bay where we could look far across the shining "open" of the Georgian Bay, "you ought to go to a point I know where I take my folks on picnics. It's up from Beausoleil Island a piece. It will cost you a dollar extra, each way. But it has more blueberries than any other I ever heard of hereabouts. The Indians never picked berries on it because it was supposed to be haunted or something, and they never went near it."

"Take us there," we agreed.

There are cottages on nearly every point of the Georgian Bay, but far in through the channels we came to an inner point, a withdrawn and rather rough and homely point where there was nothing but rude, jagged rocks and burnt-over woods and dead trees sticking up in all directions.

"Here she is," said the skipper. "Not very handsome, but lousy with blueberries."

And with promises to return a little before twelve o'clock, he putt-putted noisily away.

We scrambled up the rowdy rocks. Literally, the point was burdened with blueberries. Maybe three hundred yards this point juts out from that vast and practically uninhabited mainland of the Parry Sound country of rock and scrub and little hidden lakes and beaver meadows. A blueberry paradise.

"Jimmie," I said, between munches of the first handful, "don't let us start right here. As a couple of old blueberry pickers, let us survey the land and find one of those mossy crevices hedged about with two-foot blueberry bushes where we can actually recline at our ease and pick and eat without moving except by either crawling or rolling over."

"I know the kind of place," agreed Jim, stooping for another fistful. And so stooping and pausing and staring and walking, we surveyed the point. There were rock gullies and little rock cliffs, little clumps of woods and sheltered spaces all clad in deep bronzy green moss. And around those little clumps of bushes and along the shady margins of those damp mossy carpets the blueberry bushes were massed and dense. And they glowed with a million fat jewels of dusky blue.

"Let's start here," cried Jim, finding a little island of birch and pine about the size of a street car, which was entirely surrounded by a ten-foot margin of moss. And the hedge of bushes around the copse was like a belt of azure.

"This is the place," I admitted, kneeling down on the moss.

"You take this side," said Jim. I'll go around to the far side."

And around he vanished.

"How is it over there?" I called.

"Just about the same as your side," said Jim.

There were both kinds. The higher bushes were the bright blue kind. And hidden in amongst, the taller blue bushes were the squatter bushes of the big, succulent, black huckleberry. You would take three handfuls of the blue and follow with one of the black. Some of the black ones were as big as grapes.

"Um-yum," I said, loud enough for Jim to hear.

"Slurp, slurp," said he. I use the word slurp, but it hardly conveys the astonishing and slightly disgusting sound Jimmie made as he picked, unseen by me, on the far side of the little copse.

"Mind your table manners, Jimmie," I said.

"Swush, swush, swush," retorted Jimmie, from beyond the bushes.

"Boy," I said, "you ought to come around to this side."

"Whoosh," replied Jim.

I thought how curious it is: you know a man for years and years, and all of a sudden he comes out with some curious and hitherto undetected habit.

"Jim," I said, through a full mouth, "it may have been funny the first time you smacked your lips like that, but it is getting a little on my nerves."

"Squish, squush, slurp, whooof!" retorted Jim.

"Aw, cut it out," I retorted, and hinched myself another yard along the hedge. Ah, such berries. Now I was abreast of a three-foot-high dense hedge that positively sagged with the vivid blue ones, big as alleys, clustered like grapes, cool to the touch, cool and firm and thin-skinned.

"Ah, yum-yum," I confessed, making a little racket myself.

The sun grew warmer. I began to fill up. I could hear silly old Jim working his way around to meet me. And he was slurping.

"Jim," I begged. "For goodness sake. You're awful."

It was at the next hitch I took of a yard further along the bush that I saw Jimmie was wearing a fur hat. I was mildly surprised, because at the moment my eyes were gloatingly beholding surely the greatest blueberry bush ever seen in the history of Canada. It was four feet high, it was laden, as if with blue dew, and deep within its stems I beheld the darkly glowing shapes of scattered huckleberries of a size I had never seen before. My mind was divided between these two spectacles—the greatest berry bush in the world, and Jim wearing a silly fur cap in the middle of summer.

Finally, with a sudden tiny tingling of my scalp, I withdrew my fascinated mind away from the berry bush to deal exclusively with Jim's fur cap.

And I saw, to my intense astonishment, that Jimmie's fur hat had movable ears.

"Not To Endanger You"

I stood up.

So did the bear.

With its short front legs held quaintly before it, and its head cocked on one side, it surveyed me across the bushes.

It was a youngish bear. It was about my size. It was glossy black, with brown ruchings, and its mouth was slightly open in a friendly grin. Frothy blueberries fringed its deckle-edged lips.

"Er—hello?" I said.

"Squish, squish," replied the bear, swallowing. I could see it was not as surprised as I. I was not wearing a fur cap.

"Where's Jimmie? Mr. Frise?" I asked weakly.

"Mmmfff," said the bear, cocking its head on the other side.

"You-hoo, Jimmie?" I inquired, not very loudly.

"Sniff, sniff, " said the bear, looking away to one side, as if not knowing exactly what to do.

"Oh, Jimmie?" I repeated, just a little louder. "Are you there?"

The bear looked at me again, and I detected a more serious expression in its small, twinking eyes.

"Nice berries," I said, conversationally. I was backing slowly across the moss to where my boots, hat and coat lay piled.

The bear disappeared by dropping on to his four feet. I backed more quickly. The bear appeared at the corner of the bush and again stood up. His stomach hung very low.

Without removing my eyes from him, I stooped and fumbled for my boots and clothes. I continued backing.

The bear was now looking, with an expression of immense satisfaction, at the very large patch of berries I had discovered at the same instant I had discovered him.

I half turned and backed quartering away.

The bear dropped down and sat, as I had sat, before that shrine of blue. I turned and ran. In my stocking feet I ran, careless of the hot and ragged rock. Up a cliff or two and down a couple of gullies I scrambled. Looking back, I could see the bear sitting, like a schoolboy, before that feast of blue.

No sign of Jim. I felt badly to have left him. Where could he be? Had he tired of the plenty and gone wandering farther inland? I decided to avoid endangering him with shouting. I decided to go right out to the end of the point and wait for him.

When I came to the rough headland of the point, there, on the outermost pinnacle of the rock, ready to jump into the blue Georgian Bay, was Jimmie, looking fearfully up at me.

"Jim!" I accused. "You left me without a sign of warning."

"He came out of the bushes just as I left you to take the other side of the patch," said Jim. "So I just went right on walking."

"You did, eh?"

"I decided not to endanger you by shouting," said Jim.

"You did, eh?"

"I decided to come out here and wait for you," said Jim.

So we both waited, right out on the very little end point of rock, until the boss man came for us at twelve sharp.

Touts

August 24, 1935

"If," said Jimmie Frise, "we could only think of a racket."

"Mmmm?" said I.

"The only people making money nowadays," went on Jimmie, "are people with rackets. Plain ordinary business no longer pays. You have to have a racket."

"Oh, I know lots of plain businesses that are doing all right," I corrected. "Stores, restaurants, nice little factories."

"No, you don't," stated Jimmie. "They look all right, maybe, but they are worried sick, they haven't any money, they can't collect their accounts. They're worried sick."

"Maybe so," I said.

"But the boys with the rackets," gloated Jim, "ha, they're doing all right. By rackets I don't mean anything illegal. I mean legal rackets. Schemes by which you can shake down people in distress. The greater the distress the easier the racket."

"Such as?" I inquired.

"I don't like to name any," said Jim, guardedly, because he knows I sometimes quote him. "But when peo-

"I could feel them both looking at me, so I waved my cigar and casually sauntered up and down . . ."

ple need money badly, they can always be soaked. Or when people are afraid of falling or losing their business, they can always be taken for a ride. Strange as it may seem, when the world is poorest, the pickings are easiest."

"It doesn't make sense," I protested. "Nobody has any money these days."

"Don't be silly," scoffed Jim. "The banks are fuller of cash than they have ever been. A larger percentage of people may be out of work. But the great majority of the people, all those tens of thousands of people living in all those long, long streets of comfortable homes we pass every day, all those tens of thousands who still ride to work in crowded street cars and congest the main streets with motor traffic every morning—all those people have plenty."

"Isn't there a depression?" I wanted to know.

"They call it that," said Jimmie. "But as a matter of fact, people are merely holding tighter to what they have. I know a man that makes stationery. He tells me there has been an enormous increase in the consumption of those little black note books men carry in their pockets to itemize expenses in. Enormous increase. I know men that used to leave a dollar tip for the waiter when they took their family downtown to the hotel for Sunday dinner and even forgot to feel big by the time they walked out the door. Now they leave 15 cents and carefully itemize it in the little black book. To tip, 15 cents; like that."

"How disgusting," I agreed.

"In the good old days," went on Jim, "people threw their money around because they knew there was lots more where that came from! But, all of a sudden, everybody got scared. You've seen chickens suddenly take fright, haven't you, and seen them start running all ways for cover, when there was no apparent reason for it? Well, that's just what happened to us. We're human, just like chickens. A few years ago we got one of our periodic frights over nothing. Everybody ran indoors, locked and barred the door, and now we are hanging on to our possessions grimly in the dread fear that somebody, maybe the man next door, is going to try and take it from us.

Everybody has plenty. We are merely clutching it tighter than usual."

To Loosen Things Up

"Then how do you racket it away from them?" I inquired.

"By scaring them further," said Jim. "By showing them ways to make their money safer. And so doing, take it from them."

"I can't think of any racket along that line," I confessed.

"Neither can I," said Jimmie. "But I wish I could. I'm tired of working for my living. I'd like to be one of those fellows that just sits in a swell office and thinks."

"All the stories I've read," I submitted, "about racketeers shows that they started with a little racket and then worked up to the bigger rackets. For example, a big millionaire bootlegger started as a book salesman. Don't you know any little rackets? Haven't you heard of any ordinary little everyday rackets around the poolrooms or race tracks?"

"Ah, yes," laughed Jimmie. "Of course. Touts, you mean."

"What are touts?"

"Well, for instance," explained Jim, "there are six horses in a race, see? The tout works fast. He selects six sappy-looking individuals and approaches each one. He asks each one for a match. Then he starts in and tells them he is the brother of the jockey riding one of the horses in the next race. He gives each sap a different horse. He tells them the horse can't fail, because they are letting his brother win the race in order to get married."

"Well?" I prodded.

"Naturally, one horse has got to win that race," said Jim. "And when the race is over, the tout rushes to the man he gave the winning horse to, and generally, the sap is so delighted, he gives the tout a ten spot. Or maybe more. I knew a tout once that used this old gag and the man he tipped off bought him a $2 ticket on the horse in gratitude. The horse won and paid $150 for the $2 ticket. Nobody was more amazed than the tout."

"Jim," I said reflectively, "that sounds to me like a real racket. It is merely telling a story, that's all. You tell a story to six men. I bet you and I could make a nice thing out of touting. At last you can start making something out of the race tracks, which have been costing you plenty for years."

"Touts," explained Jimmie, "are a rather low grade of bums."

"All the better," I cried. "If two respectable-looking fellows like us went in for it, it would raise the standard of touting and we'd make a lot more money. We would be brokers, not touts. Just like the brokers, we would recommend certain investments in horses, and as the brokers make money out of the buying and selling of stocks, we would make our money out of the gifts of grateful people to whom we gave the right tip."

"But you'd be giving the wrong tip," cried Jim, "to half a dozen others!"

"Once," I continued, "we have mastered the technique of race track touting, we can go into it on a larger scale.

"I think we ought to look into ways and means of making easy money. Not for the money's sake, but to loosen things up. The more we shake people loose from their money, the sooner money will start to circulate and hard times end. Let us go into this thing on good moral grounds."

"All racketeers do," said Jim. "Meanwhile, let's go out of town to the races. Nobody would know us."

"I could wear my yellow vest," I pointed out. "It gives me a very horsey look."

One Sportsman to Another

"By jove," cried Jim. "I've got it! You be the owner of a horse. I'll speak to the saps and tell them that the gentleman with me, in the yellow vest, owns the horse. I'll tell each one you own a different horse, see? You can be standing off a little to one side, keeping your mouth shut, with your mouth kind of clamped tight, and a beady look in your eyes, like horse owners have. And you can stand sort of gazing across the race track, as if you hadn't a friend in the world, and didn't want one. That's the way horse owners look. And I'll step aside in each case, borrow a match, and then tip him off that my friend, there, you, in the yellow vest, are about to clean up. It's in the bag. It's all arranged with the stewards and the jockeys and everybody. It's your turn to win, see?"

"Jim, how perfect," I said. "And people wouldn't have the nerve to give you, the friend of the owner, a mere five spot."

"I'll laughingly tell them," said Jim, "to buy me a ticket for the tip. One sportsman to another, you know. In that way, my dear boy, we will have a winner in every race."

Thus we went out of town to the races.

My yellow vest, which I bought for beagling by mistake, certainly gave me a beautiful horsey look. I bought three cigars and hung my field glasses over my neck and threw a raincoat over my arm.

"You look like the Agha Khan himself," cried Jim triumphantly, as he received me into his car for the drive.

The first race, we did no work, because Jim said it would be better if we just paraded up and down in the crowd, letting everybody have a good look at me, while he kept his eye peeled for saps. He could pick the saps out by the way they looked at me. If they gaped sort of respectfully at me, Jim knew they would be easy suckers.

"Boy," he murmured to me, after we had made a couple of grand tours of the big lawn, crowded with race goers, "the place is full of saps. You ought to see the way they are gaping at you."

"I notice it myself," I said, removing the cigar and waving it about.

When the first race was over, and everybody dispersed after feeling their various disappointments, Jim started to work. He led me to the upper end of the lawn.

"Up here," he said, "I saw a well-dressed guy that looked as if he had never been at a race in his life before. But his eyes were popping with excitement. And when he saw you, his mouth fell open."

"Did he look as if he had money?" I inquired.

"No, he was one of those obscure, half shabby sort of men, who are the kind that carry $200 in their pocket all the time."

"Find him," I directed.

And it was no trouble finding him.

Moodily standing with one elbow on the picket fence, a gentleman of middle age was carefully studying his program. He was biting the end of a pencil and frowning.

As we drew near, I could see he was aware of us, and was watching us out of a corner of his eyes.

I stepped along the fence a little way, and Jim sauntered over to him to borrow a match and then they started to converse. I could feel them both looking at me, and when I turned, waving my cigar, to stare boldly up at the grandstand, as if wondering how many fools were betting my horse today, I caught a quick glimpse of the man, who was listening wide-eyed to Jimmie. And he was staring straight at me with his mouth slightly open.

Acting Like an Owner

In a few minutes, Jim left him and came back to me. We started to walk along in search of more suckers.

"How did he take it?" I asked, out of the side of my mouth.

"Like a lamb," said Jim. "He wanted to meet you, but I said you didn't care to meet people. I explained you were the typical horse owner. But he's going to bet and bet big. I laughingly told him he ought to buy me a two-dollar ticket for the tip."

Time went fast. By the time the bugle went, to call the horses out for the next race, we had only got two more prospects, one of them a fellow who wanted to split a $2 bet with Jim, and another who just looked at Jimmie all the time Jim talked and never said a word one way or the other.

"Once we get on to this thing," said Jim, "we can work faster. Anyway, there are only five horses in this race and we've got three of them planted."

"It's no good unless we have them all covered," I pointed out.

"I know, I know," said Jim.

We got a place back a bit where we could watch our contacts, especially the moody gentleman in the corner, the one who wanted to meet me.

The horses lined up. They were soon off. A race with one bet on it is exciting enough. But touts must get a great kick out of having six or seven bets in one race.

Jim cautioned me to show no excitement. Horse owners never get excited. They just stand stolidly, chewing their cigars and occasionally taking a brief glance through their field glasses. I did that.

"Paraboy, Paraboy wins," shouted Jim.

That was the horse we gave to the gentleman down in the corner.

"Let's go right down," I said.

"No, no, I'll take him off to one side," said Jim. "Because if you are the owner of Paraboy, you should be in the steward's paddock in a minute, leading out your horse.

"Oh, oh," said I, backing away.

Jim pushed through the crowd.

I saw him work his way to the corner.

I could not see the moody gentleman. He had suddenly vanished.

I saw Jim pushing rapidly back towards me through the slow moving and woe-begone throng.

"Did he skip?" I asked scornfully.

"Skip?" said Jim. "Look where I'm pointing."

I looked. Jim was pointing into the little winner's paddock where they were unsaddling Paraboy.

"Why," I said, "he's in there."

"Sure he's in there," said Jim. "He's the owner of Paraboy!"

"Jimmie," I said, "this yellow vest is awfully hot. I think I'll go around behind and take it off."

"Better than that," said Jim, "let's get to heck out of here altogether."

So we drove home along the lake, admiring the big homes and yachts of the gents.

Goose
Hangs
High

February 1, 1936

"Skis," said Jimmie Frise, "are not enough."

They're plenty." I assured him.

"Once you find the stores filled with all kinds of gadgets," said Jim, "you know skiing has arrived. For years, all that the stores sold were skis themselves, ski boots and ski poles. And skiing was nothing more than a sort of half-hearted hobby of the few. But all of a sudden, skiing takes on major proportions. It is becoming a cult. It has its uniform, its badges, its accessories. Why, I was in a little shop the other day that sells nothing but ski stuff."

"Ye Ski Shoppe?" I asked.

"No," said Jim. "It was just called Ski Art. And beside skis costing fifty bucks, made of some sacred wood found only in Lapland, they had two walls lined ten skis deep with skis of every sort and size. Big heavy jumping skis, slim, toothpick skis for racing. They had vast piles of ski jackets made of silk, satin, leather, pigskin, canvas and fur. All the colors of the rainbow. Then you could take

*Jim hung head down,
vainly attempting to
unbuckle his skiis . . .*

your pick of ski harness ranging all the way from fifty cents to twenty dollars. There were ski harnesses so perfect that all you have to do is stand still and you go shooting over the snow at sixty miles an hour."

"Pff, pff," I protested.

"Then, ski wax," said Jim. "All the way from Denmark, Norway, Sweden and Finland. They call it smearing. It comes in little tubes like shaving sticks, and in tin cans like floor wax, and in sardine tins, now that the world has gone ski nuts."

"You can't ski in the Congo," I pointed out.

"They'll be taking it up," decreed Jim. "They'll ski on the great, green, greasy Limpopo river. But there is one kind of wax for dry snow, another for wet snow, another for crusty snow and another for crinkly snow. Then there are ski poles you use for just ordinary ski-touring. And another kind for hills. Another kind for jumping and doing Hendrik Ibsens or whatever it is."

"He was a dramatist." I scorned.

"Don't tell me," cried Jim. "Let me guess. Then there are boots that lace and boots that buckle. There are boots with a great thick cowhide tongue that comes right across the front of the boot. Then there are canvas gaiters, red, white and blue. And ski mitts, ski toques, ski ensembles, scarf and belly bands. Comforters and stomachers, all knit in wild jigsaw designs."

"I like knitted things," I admitted. "Have they socks?"

"Long socks and short socks," recounted Jim, "high mitts and short mitts, fairy-light canvas mitts with leather palms, and little woollen bands to go around your head with ear flaps to keep your ears snug against your head so your ears won't slow you down when you are sliding."

"It sounds nutty to me," I agreed.

"Ski nuts," said Jim. "It's worse than golf ever was, even the year of the big wind."

"What year was that?" I inquired.

"1929," said Jim. "Golf is a mere piker's game to skiing. Skiing has more gadgets than golf, tennis, lawn bowling and twinkle-twit put together."

Gadgets and Twidgetts

"What's twinkle-twit?" I begged.

"You hit a dingus with feathers," said Jim. "What you call it, badminton!"

"I kind of like the sound of skiing," I confessed.

"No sport is any good," said Jim, "unless there is a lot of gear, costume, gadgets and twidgetts to it. Like fishing."

"You said it," I agreed warmly. "But in the winter there isn't any fishing."

"Our last effort at skiing," said Jim, "was somewhat frustrated by our attempt to keep pace with the young. I suggest if we do any, we get right away from the young people. The very sight of them, so muscular, so smooth and graceful, seems to dampen our spirits right at the start."

"We could sneak off somewhere," I suggested.

"I have in mind," said Jim, "up around Belfountain. It will be grand to see a trout stream in winter, even if we come to grief on skis."

"Jim, I appreciate this," I informed him. "I think we have a memorable weekend in view."

"I'll borrow one of the daughter's skis for you again?" asked Jim.

"If you please," I said. "And I'll attend to the gadgets myself."

"We'll shop together," suggested Jim.

Thus we bought ski boots made so heavy, as the young gentleman explained, that no matter what you did you couldn't land upside down. And we bought ski pants of a material so light, so windproof, so warm, that really you would think you had no pants on at all. And ski jackets, mine yellow, Jim's red, that were a joy to wear, and so like the Olympic games advertisements did we look. And elbow high mitts, and a tiny woollen headstrap to keep our ears streamlined, and a canvas black cap like a brakeman's. And ski wax, of several kinds, I favoring light fluffy snow and Jim, being more pessimistic by nature, favoring slushy, wet snow.

The only way to go skiing is to start at daybreak Saturday morning, after a large breakfast of ham and eggs, plum jam and thick toast. I am told the proper thing for a ski breakfast is a box of sardines. But with our breakfast stowed, Jim and I, scorning all questions from our various children of ski age, drove off for Belfountain. Soon the gray sludge and slush of Toronto was blooming into the glittering white snow of Halton county.

"We Canadians," said Jim, "should sooner or later realize our affinity with northern nations and races, and drop from our hearts all memory of sultry southern climes. Do you realize that our clothes here in Canada are designed by Americans? And that the clothing trade centres in St. Louis?"

"Preposterous," I assented.

"Our clothes," declared Jim, "should be designed no farther south than Inverness or Stornoway. If we want to stay British, the least we should accept in the way of clothing, is what the Scotsmen of the north wear. Imagine us Canadians slowly congealing in garments and textiles decreed by gentlemen in St. Louis, Mo.?"

"Utterly absurd," I agreed.

"These Norwegians," said Jim, "are, latitudinally speaking, our brothers."

"I'm not much on sardines," I protested. "And I should admit right away that I prefer the violins of Italy to the bagpipes of Ross and Cromarty."

The Real Color of Canada

The white landscape wheeled past, the beautiful bare barns, the bleak and desolate homes of our country cousins staring haggardly from the pinched fields. Fences wove away, and dark patches of evergreens made color against the dazzling pale morning sky.

"The real color of Canada," said Jim, gazing at it appreciatively. "Our artists wait patiently, and then go mad for a few days, painting what they pretend is Canada. For eight brief weeks in summer, they paint like fury, getting the lush greens, the gay blues of water and sky. But they ignore the true Canada. The Canada of grays and grims, and pallid leadens and faded yellows and browns."

"You mean our artists should paint like those dull Flemish and English painters, in dampish, wet grays, grayish greens?"

"Not at all," said Jim. "There is nothing dampish about our grayness. Our country is under a harsh, livid light. But there is no excuse for artists hiding in fear from Canada, the way it is for nearly ten months of the year, in order to paint it only in the brief summer and in the briefer autumn."

"They paint snow," I protested.

"Pink snow, mauve snow," said Jim. "But snow is mostly gray, platinum, grim."

"And splendid," I said.

"And terrifying," said Jim.

We were now climbing the Caledon mountain, and the highway sloped skyward; a chill came with every leap of the car over the snowy pavement; the morning blue was changing to a platinum sky, and there was a sense of shadow across the great valley behind us.

"Terrifying?" I laughed.

"Why," asked Jim, "do we Canadians huddle along the southerly border of our great land? Why do our artists avoid, with furtiveness, the truth of our magnificent country? Why has no musician written us a noble symphony, a tone poem, even?"

"We're young," I explained.

"Because," said Jim, menacingly, "all these great north lands are the last refuges of the mysterious, the magical, the dread. Because in Canada, as in Norway and Finland, there are trolls, like in Peer Gynt; and little people, such as the Irish dream about; and goblins and banshees; because Thor and Wotan are the gods of this vast country; because it is a land of legends where there are no legends yet; because, in the face of this country, artists are struck helpless."

"Pooh," said I.

"Why do we cuddle to our hearts the folk tales of those safe and sane little countries from which we came?" asked Jim. "Because we are afraid to sing our own songs. Why do we all try to love Canada with the love an Englishman has for England, or a Scotsman for Scotland or

67

an Irishman for Ireland? Why don't we love Canada the way a Canadian must love Canada?"

"Why?" I inquired, looking about at the fields which spread away at the top of Caledon Hill.

"Because," hissed Jimmie, "because we are afraid to!"

There lay the gullies with their dark and forbidding cedars. There lay the rolling hills, with their small, unpainted farm houses and barns. There lay the bleak skylines. And the snow was not really white. It was only pallid.

"I love Canada," I stated.

"You love it best," sneered Jim, "when it looks most like Ireland or Scotland."

"I love it the way it is," I said. But as I spoke, the wind picked up a large ghostly wisp of snow and whirled it around into a shape, a phantom, which swept down upon us and engulfed the car, making a hissing sound on the windows, and causing Jim to wobble the steering gear.

"See?" said Jim, in a low voice. "What do you suppose that was?"

"Pooh," I laughed.

"The Indians," said Jim, "used to call that a Wendigo. They knew what it was."

"Where do we turn in here for Belfountain?" I inquired. "Let's see what a dear familiar trout stream looks like in winter?"

But Jim's words had caused the day to take on a gloomy and desolate aspect, and I leaned back and watched the passing landscape with troubled eye. It really was rather depressing.

Across every field we passed were the shining tracks of skis. And though it was only Saturday morning, we saw groups of cars parked, and across the ski-line, parties of skiers filed, each bearing a little knapsack, heading away for some sequestered glen of cedar where they could make a fire and boil a pail of tea, and eat their onion and cheese sandwiches.

Whirling Snow Ghosts

At last we drew aside at a lonely spot, where, in the

distance, limestone cliffs rose darkly up, and half-hidden patches of sombre cedar told of hills and rolling country. And we slid out our skis, and buckled on our harness, and climbed barb wire fences and commenced a ski-tour.

Jim led. We toiled up slopes and slid down slopes. We came upon a chime of two or three hundred snow buntings, silent, faintly chippering little birds that rose like blown leaves off the snowy fields, to suddenly chop down again to earth, as if they were all connected by invisible threads. We followed them a mile, watching them rise and pitch down, and some of the sinister aspect of our native land was softened by these small buffy white creatures.

We startled out a couple of big jack rabbits—immigrants like us from the Old Country—and with comically narrow backsides, they leaped with terror away from us, keeping straight on until they had crossed the farthest sky line.

"If we humans," said Jim, resting, "find it hard to love Canada as it really is and spend so much time trying to imagine it otherwise, what about those poor jack rabbits, designed for the soft and humid climate of England, being dumped down here to make a fresh start."

"Yet they grow bigger here than they do in England," I stated.

"Maybe they have to," said Jim grimly.

And as he spoke, from over the scrubby tree tops floated, on wide wings, a gray-colored hawk, large, sinister, its beak tucked under its chin, and its baleful eyes staring downward, spying every square yard of snow. So intent was it, it did not notice us until it passed so near we heard the bitter hiss of its wings.

Jim waved his ski poles arrogantly at it and it banked wildly, as if contemplating the idea of stooping to one of us, probably the meatier of us.

"Track!" cried Jim, giving himself a scoot with his poles across the snow.

But the higher we worked, the more grim loomed the limestone cliffs, the more darkly bronzed the cedars in the gullies. The wind was rising, and the ghostly whirls of snow seemed to seek out Jim and eddy around him spectrally. He laughed.

"They're after you," I laughed back. But immediately wished I had not laughed. Because even as I laughed, the sky seemed to darken slightly, a leaden sky, with no warmth, no kindliness in it.

"Let's work to the top," shouted Jim back to me, "and then we can slide down the far side, wherever it leads, and have lunch somewhere in shelter."

"I think we have gone far enough," I called back. "I'm winded."

"Come on," shouted Jim, shoving with his ski poles.

I saw another snow ghost, larger and bigger than ever begin to gather itself, whirling and swirling madly, like a Dervish, and I paused to watch it. Straight at Jim it spun, growing bigger; and spectral arms seemed to reach out from it. I could almost hear a faint moaning sound from it. . .

"Jim," I called sharply.

But with another shove, he plunged forward. The snow ghost caught him, wound itself around him. And then. . .

Jim vanished.

Vanished right off the pallid face of the earth. He faded, as the snow wraith embraced him. It passed. And Jim was gone.

I stood rock-still for a moment, blinking my eyes and swallowing. I tried to call. No sound came. I shoved myself, with a heavy effort, a few feet forward. Then my voice returned and I shouted: "Jim."

No answer. The white unbroken expanse of snow lay featureless except for the tracks of Jim's two skis. And there they ended. The tracks just stopped.

Immensity, chill and dreadful and silent, surrounded me. Should I go forward and examine the snow for signs of giant wings? Or giant cloven hooves? Should I look for eagle marks as of some great god's helmet?

I decided not. I decided the best thing to do was turn down hill and slide as fast as skis would carry me. And then, with plenty of loud, noisy, hearty help, make a search for Jim, if search were of any avail.

But turning on skis is not easy. I was in process of turning, when I heard a faint call.

"Jim?" I replied.

"Hoy," came the faint cry.

I slithered up the slope. Unseen from where I had stood, was a sudden sharp declivity and a limestone cleft, of which there are any number in the Belfountain neighborhood.

And in that cleft, hung by his skis in the limbs of leafless and stunted oak tree, was Jimmie, head-down, vainly attempting to unbuckle his ski harness.

"Just a moment, my lad," I shouted heartily, removing my skis and clambering down into the crevice. And in a couple of moments, Jim fell heavily to the snow, beneath, uninjured but a little red in the face.

So we finished the climb, rode Valkyrie-like down into the farther valley, built a fire and boiled a pail of tea and had onion sandwiches and Norsk cheese.

"Jim," I said, as we sat on the bench made of skis and poles, "I see color in snow. I see mauve and pink."

" I don't," said Jim.

"The country is full of color." I cried. "Why, it's just a splendor of green and blue and gray and mauve and . . ."

"White," said Jim.

Weekend Party

July 4, 1936

"You're coming up," said Jimmie Frise, "to my cottage this weekend."

"Muskellunge," I asked, "or bass?"

"Both," said Jim. "I have a letter here from the family saying that a great big monster has been rolling every morning out in front of the cottage not fifty yards off shore. They say it will go twenty pounds."

"They'll have it before we get there," I suggested.

"They are saving it for you," said Jim, kindly. "We can have a grand time." We'll get there about five p.m. Saturday and go straight out fishing. All we have to do is push the skiff out from the dock and start casting right off our beach. It is grand musky water. Then, we can take the outboard and scoot down about a mile and a half to a gravel point where the bass are as thick as swallows around a barn."

"Boy, this sounds grand," I cried. "When do we have to leave there for home?"

Jim worked the cord of the motor while I bailed water out of the boat . . .

73

"We don't have to leave until after supper Sunday evening," said Jim. "That'll get us in town by midnight."

"It sounds like a real weekend," I enthused.

"I've been wanting to take you up for the past three summers," said Jim, "but somehow we never could match up our weekends. But this time you're coming."

"Sure I'm coming," I declared. "That musky rolling out in front of the cottage has got me. What bait do you generally use?"

"Oh, spoons," said Jim. "Cast in spoons, little brass ones, with black feathers on the hook. But bring your whole outfit. We'll go after them in a big way."

And when we set sail Saturday noon, Jim's car was so laden with boxes of vegetables and baskets of peas and all my fishing tackle that we could not see out of the rear view mirror.

"I love this weekend business," I told Jim as we lurched through city traffic heading for the broad highway. "This business of loading up supplies. It's a sort of Christmassy feeling every week. We poor husbands lonely at home, watering gardens, going to movies, sighing around the house in the heat. And then comes Saturday, and we get almost the same old feeling we used to get years ago when we were going to call on our best girl. We buy gifts. Instead of roses, we buy meat and vegetables and marshmallows and canned fruit. And with high hearts and a flush on our faces, we head for the wilderness, where our dear ones, amid the cool and pleasant wilderness, have hardly thought of us all week."

"I wonder," said Jim, "if other parts of the world are as happy as Canada, in regard to summer resorts? The minute a Canadian gets enough money to buy a car, he has got to have a summer cottage."

"Imagine," I cried, "having a place to park our families in summer where there are great big muskies and tough fighting bass right off the front porch! How many muskies did you get last year, by the way?"

"Oh, you know me," said Jim. "I talk a lot about fishing and I buy a lot of tackle, and I plan to go fishing a lot. But I don't really fish much. But the time I get to the cottage, I want to lie in the hammock."

Eager and Gay

"Not this weekend, my boy," I assured him. "You're with a real fisherman this time."

"That's what I need," agreed Jim. "Somebody to egg me on."

"Listen, we'll pull up in front of your cottage," I planned, "and unload the tackle out of the car straight into the skiff and push right off? Is it a bet?"

"You're on," agreed Jim delightedly.

So we arrived at the broad highway and began the four-hour battle. All bright and gay, the country smiled encouragingly as thousands of us debilitated city dwellers fought our way north, east and west. Good cars and old cars, cars laden with provender and cars loaded with mattresses, camp cots and tents; trucks grinding their obstructive way while long lines of us sweatily horned and tooted and glared sideways back at them while we passed; sport models full of superior and carefree youth that zipped by us more sedate citizens; tieups, old junk cars coughing up hills; ah, the parody of Saturday afternoon. If it were not that we were as bridegrooms, if we were not eager and gay, we would never so much as take our cars out of the garage of a Saturday afternoon.

But Jim drove and cussed and sneered; and I leaned out the window and shouted uncomplimentary remarks to drivers of less agile craft than ours; or retorted to the jeers of others whose cars were more agile than ours. And in due time we came to the end of pavement, and launched forth into a highway of gravel, where we ate dust, and skittered and bumped over washboards, and finally left even the gravel to take to a narrow little backwoods road where, if you meet a car coming against you, either you or it has to back up to a wide place to pass.

And about the time we struck this country road, the sky had darkened, rumbles of thunder warned of weather, and down into the leaves that brushed the sides of the car spattered the first big drops of summer rain.

"All the better for fishing," I assured Jim. "You aren't afraid of a wetting?"

"The best muskie I ever got," replied Jim, "I got in a heavy rain that made the water leap up in a million little jets."

And at six p.m. daylight saving time, in a world gray and sweeping with rain, we arrived at Jim's cottage. And from indoors, as we turned in, came a bevy of gay young people, and we unloaded the chariot and the boxes were happily hustled indoors. But I could sense a certain embarrassment. I could see them catching Jim's eye and giving him signals. And in a few minutes Jim came out heartily and said:

"They've got some kids staying with them, so I guess it's the tent for us two old campaigners."

"Grand, Jim," I cried. "I love the sound of rain on a tent."

"We had better put it up now, rather than when we come in from fishing." suggested Jim.

"Right-o," said I.

But then we were called for supper, and by the time supper was over and I looked out across the dimpling water, where the rain still slanted and peppered, it seemed to be getting a little dark.

"Jim," I said, "let's slam the tent up or we won't get out to-night."

Caulking the Old Boat

Jim went hunting and came back with a roughly-bundled tent of an oldish grayish color, and then we both hunted for the poles which never turned up.

"We can cut poles in a jiffy," said Jim. Which we did, and they weren't very good poles. We unrolled the tent and figured it all out, and struggled with the poles and the billowy canvas, and the rain still spattered and slanted. We had to go and cut pegs for the guy-ropes of the tent, and it got darker all the time.

"Just cut pegs for the corners," said Jimmie. "We'll do with a rough job tonight."

"We'll never get fishing," I said. "But we can be up bright and early."

The tent was pretty damp by the time we had it more or less erected, and the ground was soaked. But Jim got camp cots out of the cottage, and presently we got to bed.

"Early to bed, early to rise." said Jim.

"The mosquitoes are fairly bad." I answered.

The sun waked us. I could tell by the angle of the sun that it was not really early. In fact, it was the voices of children in the distance, apparently in swimming, that really wakened me.

"Jim," I cried, looking at my watch, "it's after nine, daylight saving."

We leaped out of bed to find a lovely sunny morning, the water still as a mill pond, and nobody up yet.

"We'll just go in and snatch a bite of breakfast," decreed Jim. "And away."

Quietly, so as not to wake everyone, we had a bowl of dry cereal and bread and jam. And then we gathered up our tackle and headed for the little dock in front of Jim's.

"The boat," said Jim, "was kind of leaky last week but I told them to leave it in the water to soak up."

The boat, however, was on the beach, turned over. And I could see right through the cracks in the keel.

"Can we get a boat handy?" I inquired, businesslike.

"It won't take ten minutes to caulk this up," said Jim. "I brought a can of new caulking stuff for it."

Which he produced from his fishing tackle box.

"Jim," I said, "don't fool with this stuff. Let's rent one or borrow one, handy."

"The nearest place to rent one is six miles up the lake," said Jim, "and I wouldn't dream of borrowing anybody else's boat around here. Anyway, they are likely all out fishing."

"Well," said I. So I laid down all my tackle, rod cases, steel boxes, leather bags, nets, gaffs and what not, and helped Jim pry the lid off the caulking cement.

"This stuff is elastic," explained Jim happily, cutting himself a sort of spreader from a stick. "It dries quick, the man said. But it is elastic and sticks in the cracks."

The stuff was very liquid. We stirred it and spread it

carefully in the wider cracks. Then we found smaller cracks and nail holes and carefully stuffed the cement into them.

"This is a great old boat," said Jim. "I wouldn't get rid of it for any boat they make nowadays. It's a pleasure to handle this boat."

We just went on stuffing and spreading. We found some quite large holes at the ends.

"Now," said Jim, "let her dry a few minutes, and away we go."

"Let's Prove We're Anglers"

I sat down and batted mosquitoes away.

Jim walked out on the little dock. It was high and dry, and the piles of stones that supported it were at least ten feet from water's edge.

"The water in these lakes," said Jim, "is dropping every year."

"Maybe if we waited a few years," I said, "we could come up and catch the muskies on dry land."

Jim started moving stones from under the ricketty dock out towards the water. There is something attractive about moving a stone.

Jim moved about four stones. I got up and picked one up that I saw him deliberately avoid. I hoisted it. Waddled down to the water with it. Plunked it down.

"Boy," said Jim, "you've got a back."

"Short men are good at lifting," I explained.

"We might as well do this," said Jim, "while waiting for the boat to dry."

One by one, we hoisted the stones. Jim tried several, he couldn't even get knee high. I hoisted them easily.

"I never realized," said Jim graciously, "how strong you really were."

"I was always a good lifter." I assured him.

We got them all shifted. We made two good strong piles of them, and Jim said we might as well shift the planks, now that we had got the stones moved. It was only a matter of ten minutes before we had a nice little dock rebuilt, right where it should be.

We were just testing the caulking on the skiff when

78

there came a strong call from the cottage.

"Dinner!"

"Dinner." I said. And my watch showed noon.

We went up and squeezed in at a very crowded table, with several of the smaller children sitting at a side table, and had a great big summer dinner of cold meat and salad and about five cups of tea the way you can drink it at a summer resort. And it was two o'clock, daylight saving, when we walked out on the veranda, and Jim sagged into the hammock.

"Come, me lad," I laughed at him. "None of that!"

"Just for five minutes," said Jim. "Just to start digestion."

I sat and rocked while the veranda filled with youth; and old Jim, with a grin on his face, closed his eyes and enjoyed a brief snooze.

"Up you get," I commanded. "We're anglers. Let's prove it."

"Oh, me," groaned Jim, and rose heavily and went indoors to get the outboard motor. I helped him carry it down. The skiff was not yet dry. As a matter of fact, the cement only had a sort of crust on it, which broke when you stuck your finger on it, and the sticky stuff clung to your finger.

"Let her go," said Jim. "The water will harden it."

We launched the skiff, carefully.

"She leaks." I noted.

"You bail," decreed Jim. "It will close up in no time."

He adjusted the outboard, I bailed. I batted mosquitoes. The lake was glassy smooth. There was a haze. I scanned the water for the boil of a monster musky rising. But only the dip of little water flies disturbed the glassy smoothness.

Jim wound up the engine cord and jerked. The water bubbled. The engine hissed and sucked. We moved, in slow bunts, forward with each jerk of the outboard cord.

"Hm, hm, hm." said Jim, opening this and shifting that. He stuck his finger in the fuel tank and inspected the mixture. He gave little quick pulls of the cord. Long, slow hauls at it. He twiddled gimmicks and gadgets.

"Hm, hm, hm." said I.

But bailing was necessary. There were several small clear little pencils of water spouting up out of the bottom of the boat from places we had not suspected.

"Paddle her in to the dock." said Jim.

"What with?" I asked politely.

"Oh, I forgot the oars," said Jim. "Paddle her in with your bailing can."

I paddled as best I could the little distance we had drifted. Jim unscrewed the outboard and hoisted it on to the wharf.

"It won't be a second," said Jim. "I know the insides of these things like a book."

I went for a little walk along the beach while Jim took the thing apart. I came back and sat down and watched him, as he unscrewed and unbolted, examined, refitted. He got covered with black grease. He seemed so concentrated, I hated to disturb him.

He tried three different bolts in the one nut he was holding, so I said:

"Jim, it occurs to me we ought to get an early start home so as to miss that dreadful traffic. A day like this, I bet it would take seven hours to get back to town."

Jim pondered. He tried the three small bolts in two other nuts.

"Hm," said he. "What time is it?"

"It's three-fifteen."

"Not much of a day for fishing," he said, gazing at the glassy and brassy lake.

"I don't think a fish would look at a bait on a day like this," I agreed, rising. "What do you say if we get an early start and avoid the traffic jam?"

"I'm with you," agreed Jim. "I'll take this thing back to town and have it over-hauled. By next week, the boat will be thoroughly tight. We'll make a day of it next week."

We got a box and Jim put all the loose parts of the outboard in it. We packed our stuff into the car.

"I should attend to a couple of leaks in the roof," said Jim. "They were nearly flooded out last night. It wouldn't take ten minutes to slip a few shingles in under

80

the spots that leak."

"How about doing that next week?" I asked. "Time is flying. We don't want to get into that traffic jam."

We made our farewells to the one or two who were not having the afternoon siesta.

"Next week," said Jim, gazing tenderly at his cottage, the placid lake, the dock, the boat, once more upside down, its repaired bottom bright with spots of pale cement, "we'll make a real day of it."

"Yes," I said, "yes, yes, yes, yes."

Only I made each yes sound different from the others.

The fish fought hard, leaping,
diving and jerking . . .

All This Frittering

July 25, 1936

"To tell the truth," said Jimmie Frise, "I'm getting a little tired of this weekend business."

"My dear boy," I said, "on a day like this?"

"On any kind of a day," stated Jim. "We work like maniacs all week. Why? To get away over the weekend. Then we drive like maniacs for two hundred miles. Why? To reach some distant point, where we work like maniacs again to enjoy ourselves a few hours Saturday evening and part of Sunday up until about three p.m. Then like maniacs we drive home again, two hundred miles. Why? To be on time to start work again like maniacs for the next week."

"It does sound funny," I confessed.

"It is funny," said Jim, not laughing.

"But isn't this swell?" I asked, looking around at the ripe fields wheeling past the car windows, the bright summer sky, the sense of being alive that filled the whole earth. "Suppose we didn't work like maniacs, but only took life lazily all week and then took the weekends lazily, sleeping all Sunday, would that be any better?"

"How," said Jim, "about working like maniacs all week, weekends and all? How about working like maniacs straight ahead for ten years? In ten years you and I could make enough jack to retire for life."

"And die," I suggested, "of over-exertion the year after we quit?"

"Nonsense," scoffed Jim, who was driving; "that's one of those notions set at large by the big shots to keep a lot of us from trying to be big shots, too. Look around you. Look at the people that are having the good time. Every-one of them are birds who had enough sense when they were young to realize that the only way to really enjoy life was to work like fury and gather in the dough. And then they could coast."

"It's the old problem," I sighed. "To enjoy life as you go along or to toil in the vineyard and store up treasures in heaven or your fifties."

"My fifties," said Jim, "are creeping pretty nigh."

"You'll still be fond of fishing," I assured him.

"And Russian pool," sneered Jim, "and horse races and sailing and rabbit shooting and duck shooting and poker and . . ."

"I don't know anybody," I laughed, "who has as much fun as you."

"It's just frittering," declared Jim heatedly. "Fritter-ing, that's all it is. I play pool in a pool room. I go to the races and stand in the jam, I have an outboard motor. I go down around Lindsay to shoot a few rabbits. I go and sit in a frozen bog in a lake where the ducks have been shot off forty years ago by the millionaires who used to own it. Do you know what I could have, if I worked and saved my dough?"

"Stomach trouble," I said. "A sour puss. A mean disposition."

"I could play pool," said Jim, "in a swell club, with a marker in a white coat standing by to hold my cigar butt for me. I could sit in the members' enclosure at the races on an ornamental bench, with nobody standing in front of me. I could own a yacht, a sailing yacht, and go on cruises down the St. Lawrence."

The Whole Secret

"Would you invite me?" I asked.

"Instead of frittering a Saturday," said Jim, with an expression so hard that I knew my old friend, if he ever changed, would invite a far better class of people than I on his yacht, "instead of dashing down to a swamp near Lindsay to shoot maybe one rabbit. I could go to the Rockies on a six-weeks' hunt for grizzlies, and mountain sheep and moose. Or maybe on safari to Africa after big, dangerous game."

"Look at Hemingway," I said. "Hemingway used to just be a plain newspaperman like us, working on The Star Weekly, and he started to work and wrote novels, and now look at him. Shooting elephants."

"Lions," said Jim. "And for duck shooting I could take a month in December and go down to the Gulf of Mexico to an exclusive club and shoot a thousand mallards."

"By the time you had made enough money to do all this," I explained, "you would be changed. You wouldn't want to do anything so silly as shoot and fish and go to races. You would only want to do something sensible, like building a bank or buying a mine or a railroad."

"You can't take out of a man," said Jim, "the things the Lord put into him first."

"That's the whole secret," I agreed. "And the Lord put little pleasant things in us, like wanting to be happy and fish and go motoring in the country like this. Or shoot rabbits. If the Lord had put into us the desire to shoot lions or sail yachts He would have fitted us up with the steam for making big money."

"Right there," said Jim sharply, "I disagree. It is all a case of taking the easiest course. You and I could make money as easy as any broker or shirt maker. But we would have to work. We'd have to give up all these silly weekends. We'd have to sell our rods and guns and stuff. We'd have to buckle down."

"With a goal in view," I agreed, "I could work as hard as any man."

"All my life," said Jim, "I have smiled at these big shots who work like fools, scorning the little amusements of life. But now I am beginning to think the smile has been on me. How many fish have we got this year for all the trips we've taken?"

"Its been an off year," I admitted.

"Its been an average year," stated Jim. "I bet we haven't got forty trout apiece, and so far about fifteen bass apiece."

"I nearly got a muskie week before last," I reminded him. "Remember the fellow who got that twelve-pounder just ahead of me? If he hadn't been there I'd have got that muskie."

"We fished trout every weekend in May and June and bass and muskies ever since," said Jim. "Do you realize that if we had the spondoolicks we could go to places where we could catch forty trout in an evening and fifteen bass in one hour?"

"It would be illegal," I pointed out.

To Be Big Shots

"What would we care," cried Jim, "if we were big shots? No, sir. Down where we can get on our frittering little trips everything we want has been gone years ago. But out in the distant places, far beyond the reach of anybody but the rich, there is everything we want. Grizzlies in Alaska. Lions in Africa. All the wide sea to sail in. Lovely, strange countries we will never see. Secret, lovely places like Greenland; and we feel excited going to Muskoka in January. Places that make you cry just to look at them, like Rome. And we get a big kick out of Niagara Falls."

"I guess the ones born in Rome don't cry," I supposed, "and when they get a picture postcard of Niagara Falls they put it up on the wall and keep it for thirty years."

"You have been filled," declared Jimmie, "with the

bunk that is taught by the big shots for the purpose of keeping you happy and out of the running. Suppose we all tried to get rich? How would the big shots like that? So they teach us to sing 'There Is No Place Like Home.' And they go to Africa."

"Jim," I accused, "you're a Communist."

"I am only sore," said Jim, stamping on the gas and shooting the car recklessly past a string of slow-goers, "at all this piddling around and never getting anywhere. I'm sick and tired of it. I feel as if I never wanted to go on another weekend. I feel like cutting out all this trifling and getting down to work. I'd like to have about two hundred thousand dollars."

"How could you make that," I inquired, "in ten years?"

"By working," said Jim. "And saving. And putting every cent away except what I really need to live on. Capital is the secret. Capital begets capital. Money works. The more I saved the smarter I would get at making it. The more money I had the more I would mix with men who make money and they would inspire fresh ideas in me. I could think up marvellous advertising art. I could presently found a company for producing advertising art of a new and sensational kind. The money I make I would invest in other companies that I would know, from my wealthy friends, were money makers. We're saps."

"I could write novels," I submitted, "and movie scenarios. I've heard of men making a hundred thousand dollars out of a movie scenario. Two of those and I'd have two hundred thousand. And in less than ten years."

Jim drove in silence, with a fierce expression on his face. I sat thinking of writing two movie scenarios.

"All right," said Jim suddenly. "I'm set. I tell you, this is the last trip. If it weren't for you I'd turn right around now and go back home and head straight for the office."

"Don't mind me," I assured him. "If you really are convinced, Jim, I would be only too glad to join you. These great resolutions come like this. It's a sort of spiritual thing. You suddenly see things clear and plain. Turn at the next corner."

"Are you with me?" asked Jim, his face strained with the depth of his feeling. "Do you feel as I feel? Are we fools? Shouldn't we cut out all this frittering and get down to work? Shouldn't we make hay while the sun shines and be free men, in a few years, to go where we like, to the ends of the earth, to where there is fun and beauty and life?"

"Turn at the next crossroads, Jim," I said breathlessly.

Seeing a Great Light

"What a sap I have been," groaned Jim, shifting restlessly and gripping the steering wheel with excitement. "Don't ever speak to me of weekends again," he cried. "Don't ever try to show me a snapshot of a fish."

"I'm changing, too," I reminded him. "No more snapshots."

We came to a crossroads. Just a country concession road. Jim put out his arm to warn the long parade of weekend traffic. He swung the car into the little dirt road.

"Take your time," I warned. "No gap in traffic in sight yet."

"Here's a car coming out," said Jim. And he drove his car a few rolls farther down the dirt road to let pass a gaudy-looking green car that was coming out to the highway.

But the outcoming car halted and a man stepped out of it.

"Are you going in to Camp Cumfy Duck?" asked this gentleman, who was sunburned and jolly looking and wore a linen cap.

"No, sir, we're not," said Jim politely, but in the manner of a man who knows his own mind.

"Sorry," said the linen-capped gent, eyeing our fishing tackle and gear. "Going fishing?"

"No, sir, we're not," said Jim, in the same presidential manner.

"I've come away," explained the tanned gentleman, "with the favorite lure of the head guide at Camp Cumfy Duck, and I was hoping you were headed in there to save us a nine-mile drive back. Ever been to Camp Cumfy Duck?"

"Never," said Jim, as if the interview were now ended.

"Greatest muskie water in Canada," said the genial fellow, heartily. "You look like a couple of sports, or I wouldn't mention it. Wait a second."

He skipped around the back of the car and lifted the lid of a rough box leaking ice water.

He hauled forth a muskie of at least twenty pounds. It was jade green. It was barred with deep shadows of darker jade. It was square-built and powerful. Its immense jaws were fanged with pearly white scimitars. Its baleful eye was proud and fierce, even in death.

Jim got out one side of the car and I the other.

"How much?" asked Jim.

"Twenty-one pounds," said the sportsman, and his partner, a lean man, got out and joined us at the back of the car.

Out of the ice packing our new friend drew forth five more muskies, eight-pounders, ten-pounders, twelve-pounders.

"All taken," he stated proudly, "on the Tipsy Giggler. A very sporting bait. Single hook."

"Very," Jim and I both agreed, hefting the fish. "Very."

We laid them out on the grass by the roadside. We admired them and measured them. We lifted them up and laid them down.

"Camp Cumfy Duck?" said Jim. "I never even heard of it."

"You never hear of the good places," said our friend. "The only places you ever hear of are the ones that have to be heard of or else nobody would go, since the fish are all gone."

"That's true," said Jim, as if seeing a great light. "By jove, that's a fact. You said it.

"As a matter of fact," I said, "we were looking for some likely spot to spend the weekend. I wonder would there be room at Camp Cumfy Duck for us?"

"My dear sir," said the new found friend, "I'll give you

a note to the proprietor!"

So while Jim and I lifted the fish reverently back into the ice box the man in the linen cap wrote a note on a scrap of paper.

And down the side road we drove, eight bumpy, swampy miles, to a pleasant old summer hotel on a quiet reedy lake where islands and patches of rushes showed where the muskies rolled and fed of an evening.

We had a quick supper. We shoved off in a skiff. We coasted past the first patch of reeds, I in the stern, Jim in the bow, casting. With Tipsy Gigglers.

"There was really no use turning back," said Jim, "not when there were muskies so handy. But this is good-by."

Jim sped his lure like a bullet deep into a pocket among the rushes. I cast mine high and true across the far end of the reed patch. We started to draw the lures home. A sound like a calf falling in the water attracted my attention to Jim's lure, where an enormous boil in the water indicated trouble.

"Sock him!" I shouted. Jim socked. A huge crocodilian form of jade green leaped tumultuously out of the reedy water.

"Jim," I roared, "it's the fish of your life."

I felt a violent jag at my rod. I looked. Another vast boil in the water appeared just about where my lure would be. I struck.

Out, waggling heavily from side to side, came another monstrous muskie, his jaws agape, to flounder with my Tipsy Giggler dangling from his lip.

"Farewell," roared Jimmie. "Hello!"

And of the perils we met and mastered, the dreadful rushes of those simultaneous fish, their dives into the reeds, their leaps high into the air on the end of our fragile lines, the times they went under the boat, the times they sulked and the times they raced, I will not detail; because matters of this kind are of interest only to those who wield the dainty four ounce casting rod in the face of the tiger of all fishes.

But we got them. We got them, Jim gaffing mine, holding his doggo meantime then I gaffed his. And we shook hands a score of times and shouted and sang, and rowed back to Camp Cumfy Duck, vowing never would we leave it for any lesser kingdom of the blessed.

And when, long after gutting and icing our great fish, we retired to bed hoping for tomorrow, I said to Jimmie:

"Look here: how about this frittering business? This conversion? Going after big money?"

"Fate," said Jim, sleepily, "must have overheard us."

Guides
$5.00
Per Day

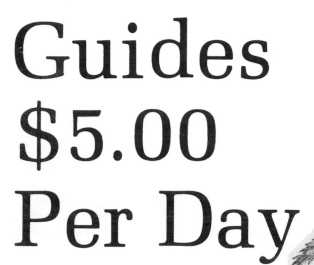

July 24, 1937

With a sudden thud and lurch, we leaped into the white water. "Oar, oar," I heard Jim roar above the hiss and thunder of the rapids . . .

"How much dough," asked Jimmie Frise, "have you got on you?"

"Two," I said, "twenty-five."

"We're in a bit of a jam," said Jim in a low voice.

"How?" I demanded indignantly.

We were sitting on the wharf of the little summer hotel to which Jimmie had inveigled me for a quick week-end on the strength of stories he had heard from a friend about the wonderful bass fishing. We had got no bass. In fact, we hadn't got anything at all. Even the birds didn't sing in this particular section of Ontario's wilds. It was one of those sandy, rocky regions, full of hay and old stump fences, in which nobody had done anything since the pioneers had first discovered its poverty seventy-five years ago. Its waters were as barren as its soil. The most you could hope for in such a country was sunburn.

"What kind of a jam?" I demanded, none too amiably.

"The bill," said Jim, "is seven dollars and a half, including boat hire. All I've got is a dollar-eighty. All you've got is two-twenty-five."

"Don't forget gas for going home," I pointed out acidly. "I provide the car and the gas. I thought at least you'd attend to the hotel bill."

"I left it in my other pants," said Jim.

"We'll tell the proprietor we'll send him the money." I suggested.

"You saw the proprietor," said Jim. "A fat chance we'd have."

"Give him a cheque," I stated.

"You saw the big sign in the hall," said Jim. " 'No cheques cashed, not even good ones'."

"Well," I said, "tell him, who we are. Explain the situation. What can he do?"

"He can make a scene," said Jim. "He's a local boy. He's got a voice full of rock and hay and west wind. He's got the temperament of a sawmill. When he throws people out of his hotel, he throws them."

"I take life as it comes," I informed Jim. "I don't mind the odd incident in my life. You've got that modern straight-line production idea of life in your system. You like life to glide smoothly. It isn't natural. If this is one of the times that life goes natural on us I'm prepared."

"You can talk," sneered Jimmie. "A little guy like you. If there is going to be any chucking out around here, who's going to get it in the seat of the pants? You or me?"

"It was you brought me here," I pointed out. "Six-pound bass. Heh, heh! Sooner or later, my friend, you will realize that there is in life a mystic law of compensation. You have to pay for everything. Sooner or later, things all balance. This jam you've got us into balances your folly in believing all that stuff about six-pound bass. Why, it stands to reason, in a country like this . . ."

"You were eager to come," protested Jim. "I merely suggested."

"Merely suggested," I shouted. "Why, you wheedled, pleaded, coaxed, cajoled, misrepresented . . ."

Our argument was interrupted by the sound of a car, and down the two sand ruts that do for a road in these parts came a magnificent vehicle. It had an American license, and on its front bumper and side fenders bulged those huge sporting bags of heavy canvas trimmed with rich leather which the Americans seem to know where to buy. The car ran slowly out on to the wharf and out of it stepped three people, two little skinny men in linen caps and linen plus fours, and a huge lady in military breeches and a gaudy sport shirt. They were all wearing dark glasses, and the skin on their noses was peeling.

"Watch Out for That Chute"

"Howdy, boys?" said the leading gentleman, a spry, silvery little fellow. "Any guides around here?"

Jim gave me a quick nudge with his heel.

"Yes, sir," said Jim, springing up. "We're guides."

I hastened to my feet, too. Jim stood in a special pose, his shoulders hunched and his arms hanging. He put a curiously dumb expression on his face and drew the back of his hand across his mouth. I followed suit. If we didn't look like guides, we felt like them. Just try it some time. Draw the back of your hand slowly across your mouth and see if it doesn't make you feel like your Uncle Hank.

"Do you know where the Indian River is?" asked the silvery little man.

"Yes, sir," said Jim; "there ain't no place around here we don't know, born and raised. And there ain't any fish we ain't personal acquainted with."

"Do you think if we stop here," asked the large lady in a deep voice, "you could show us plenty bass?"

Now, Jim had to think cautiously.

"Lady," he said, "bass is temperamental. You know that, I can see. You're a sportswoman. Some days they bite. Some days you wouldn't hardly think they was a bass in the whole country. But if you want two of the best guides in the country to show you where to fish and to carry your tackle and cook your shore dinner, at the usual rates of pay, then them two guides is standing here at your service."

"There's something," said the lady to her two companions, "strikes me about these two lads. It won't hurt us to give them a try."

"Lady," said Jim, "how would this appeal to you? Instead of going up to the hotel right off, just leave your stuff in the car and spend the day on the water. If you like the country, then stay."

"A very good idea," said the lady; and the two thin little men agreed. "We have our own outboard engine. Will you provide a boat?"

"Certainly, lady," said Jim, seeing his scheme blossoming perfectly. "We'll go git the boat now, while you decide what to take from the car."

So Jim and I hurried up to the hotel and saw the proprietor. We explained to him that a party of friends had unexpectedly turned up and we were going to stay the day instead of pushing off for home as we had intended. We wanted a square-stern skiff and lunch for five of us.

"Help yourself to the boat," said the proprietor. "Are your friends likely to stay over?"

"We'll do our best to persuade them," we assured him.

Back we hurried and Jim got the square-stern skiff out of the boathouse while I busied myself helping lift out the engine from the spacious cavern in the rear of the big car and sorted from the rich and exciting piles of dunnage the things we would want for the day's fishing. When Jim saw the hotel proprietor come out on the veranda with the big lunch basket, he ran up and intercepted him, carrying the lunch down himself.

The proprietor followed and stood watching us load the skiff, while we felt our hearts in our mouth.

"The Indian River," said the proprietor, "is the best bass fishing in the country. Go down to the second chute. You'll have to portage the first chute. Then you run about two miles. Watch out for that second chute. She's dangerous. You'll see the landing on the left-hand side. You can either portage across or just walk over the trail and fish the rocks below the chute. But she's a tough portage, so I suggest you leave your stuff this side and walk over."

Funny Streak in the Water

"The boys know the way, I suppose," said the lady, whose name we learned was Mrs. Schmaltz, of Canton, O. Mr. Schmaltz was the silveriest of the two men, the other was Mrs. Schmaltz's brother.

"You're in good hands," agreed the proprietor heartily, as Jim, who knows outboard engines, gave the rope the first twirl.

"Heh, heh," we laughed, modestly, as the skiff moved slowly out from the wharf.

And with a couple more yanks, Jim got the lovely big engine snoring and away we bore. I sat in the bow, the two thin gentlemen next, the lady in the main stern seat and Jim behind her at the engine. We were deeply loaded, but comfortable.

Now Jim and I had only a rough idea where the Indian River lay. It had been suggested to us the day before by locals, but it seemed too far to row. It was, they had indicated, in the far north-east corner of the lake, and there we headed, I as bow guide, keeping my eye on Jim and giving him little signals to starboard and port as we sped across the pleasant lake.

In due time we came into a bay and saw the timbers of an ancient log chute, and to this we steered and came without trouble to the landing for the clearly marked trail leading over the rocks and scrub.

"You folks," said Jim, "just go ahead over the trail and we'll follow with the stuff."

"This skiff," I said, "weighs about two hundred

pounds, Jim."

"I thought," said he, "that you were always ready for life, when it happened."

We tried picking it up. We tried sliding it on its keel. We tried hauling it by both of us taking the front end and dragging. We ended by going into the brush and picking up five round dead poles which we laid on the trail and rolled the skiff on them, then returning to pick up the poles and re-lay them. It was a tedious and exhausting business, but we got the skiff across.

Three return trips each accounted for the engine, the tackle boxes, rods, oars, cushions and lunch basket.

"Sorry to be so long," said Jim, as we packed the skiff. "But I always says, comfort is more than half a camping trip. None of this going light and painful."

"Let's go," said Mr. Schmaltz shortly.

In we crawled to our places in the skiff, and Jim pushed off and wound the engine into life, and down a winding rocky river we sped, while the Schmaltzes sat behind their smoked glasses, chins lifted, radiantly gazing at the godforsaken country as if it were as beautiful as the Bay of Naples. It was my job in the bow to watch ahead for shoals and not to look at the rocky shores or scenery, and I was peering alertly into the water ahead as Jim made the engine sing, when I noticed a funny thing in the water.

It was a sort of long thin streak. A sort of swirl. A kind of a little whirlpool. I raised my eyes.

Not fifty yards ahead I saw an incredible white dancing and leaping.

"The chute," I roared, standing up and waving my arms frantically.

Jim slammed the engine handle over and the skiff dipped perilously, causing me to sit down and crouch in the bow. On both sides the rocky shores rose hard and mean, with no crack or fissure in which a grip might be taken or a ship in distress beached.

Mrs. Schmaltz was sitting gripping the sides of the skiff, her face glowing and her mouth open in a kind of ecstasy. Mr. Schmaltz and the brother-in-law were half risen from their seat and their eyes were blazing with excitement. Back of them all sat Jimmie, with an expression of absolute expressionlessness on his face, bearing his weight hard over on the engine handle.

A Perfect Adventure

We did one circle. One complete circle in that smooth, oily, rushing stream, and the skiff was head on as, with a sudden surge and thud, we leaped into the white water.

"Oar, oar," I heard Jim roaring above the hiss and thunder of the rapids. I took an oar and half rose in the bow, but straight under my chin leaped giant waves and white plumes, and past the corners of my eyes flashed black wet rocks, jagged and smooth, and I felt small, sharp taps and one vast sickening thud as the skiff touched. I felt her slew slightly, then break free and continue the mad gallop. A despairing glance showed Mrs. Schmaltz still gripping the sides and lifting her chin to it as if she were a Valkyrie. Mr. Schmaltz and the brother-in-law were grinning whitely from ear to ear, half lifted, in eagerness, from the seat.

Then, with a final vast sweep and rush, the skiff plunged out into a great rolling, heaving pool. I stood up with the oar and poised myself as magnificently as I could. I plunged the oar into the coiling, heaving water. I felt the oar gripped. I put all my strength to hold it. The oar was pressed immensely against the side of the skiff. I heaved.

"Look out," screamed everybody.

Then I felt the skiff slowly lift, turn and roll over, and I was darkly and limply wallowing in the depths.

I touched bottom. I heaved up, saw air, felt air, and something clutched me.

It was Mrs. Schmaltz. Standing up to her belt in shallow water, she had me by the shirt. She was laughing and yelling. Up to their waists, staggering and laughing riotously with meaningless shouts were Mr. Schmaltz and the brother-in-law, while scampering for shore, was Jimmie. And far down the current bobbed the skiff, upside down.

The pool at the foot of the chute was shallow and gravelly, and there we waded, hunting for the lost duffle.

We got one tackle box. But the engine, the lunch, the rods, all, all were gone. The skiff grounded a little way down on the opposite shore and Mrs. Schmaltz commanded that we leave it there.

"This road," she pointed to a rough trail, "leads somewhere. We'll take it."

"But your engine!" said Jim.

"Listen," she cried, "we've been coming to Canada for thirty years. We've spent thousands of dollars on engines, camping equipment, tents, and nothing has ever happened to us."

"Nothing," shouted Mr. Schmaltz, "but mosquito bites."

"And at last," sang Mrs. Schmaltz, with a wild air, "we got wrecked in a rapids. A mighty rapids."

"A dangerous rapids," shouted Mrs. Schmaltz's brother. "Where many lives have been lost, lumberjacks and couriers de boys."

"We don't want the engine," cried Mrs. Schmaltz. "If we got the engine, it would spoil it. We want to tell our friends we lost everything. Everything but one tackle box. It's perfect. Beautiful. Magnificent. At last, after all these years, we have had an adventure. And we owe it all to you."

She beamed on us and I sat down and she came and patted my wet back.

"We've got three weeks more," said Mr. Schmaltz, very business like. "We'll hire you for the balance of our stay."

"This is terrible," said Jim. "Mister, we have signed up with a big party coming tomorrow."

"We'll arrange other guides for them," said Mr. Schmaltz, linking his arm possessively through Jimmie's.

"They're regular customers," explained Jim. "We couldn't possibly leave them. We've been guiding them twenty years. You know how it is."

So we headed out the tote road. Mrs. Schmaltz taking my elbow to help me over the rougher bits and Mr. Schmaltz and the brother-in-law giving Jim a hand over the stonier knolls, and a settler's cabin told us to keep straight on three miles to a main road where we could hire a farmer's car to take us back to the hotel.

And very proudly and tenderly we were escorted back to the hotel where, happily, we found the proprietor had gone into town for provisions. There Mr. Schmaltz paid us $5.00 each for the best day's guiding value he had ever had; and while they were shown their rooms and changed their clothes, Jim and I paid our bill—including $1 for sending for the stranded skiff—and beat it fast for fear the truth should catch us.

Cat-tail Bog

October 2, 1937

*"Hye!" roared Jim, and the punt gave
a wobble. A big fat mallard had
jumped from the bog behind us and
nearly collided with my umbrella.*

102

"At last," cried Jimmie Frise, "I have everything set to take you duck hunting."

"Not me," I assured him.

"Listen," said Jim earnestly, "I've built the swellest duck blind you ever saw. I spent the whole weekend building it. It's on the one point in the whole bog where, you might say, every duck from Hudson Bay has to pass on its way south."

"Count me out," I said.

"Now listen," said Jim, "it's the swellest blind I ever saw. It's built with poles, overlaid with cedar all woven together and cattails entirely covering it. It's so clever a blind even an old grandma duck that has been up and down America eight or ten times wouldn't suspect it."

"I'm booked up," I said, "every weekend from now to Christmas."

"Aw," said Jim, "don't be so pig-headed. You don't know what you are missing. You call yourself a sportsman? Duck shooting is the basic sport. Until you have shot ducks you're nobody in the world of outdoor sport."

"Give me," I stated, "deer, moose, bear, pheasants, partridge or porcupines. Anything dry. But deliver me from all dampness, chill, sleet, mud and east winds."

"This duck blind," stated Jim, "is practically weather proof. I built a regular little bench in it for us to sit on. I built a kind of a shelter underneath so that if we do get cold we can snuggle down under and get warm. It is made of thick cedar boughs woven in around a framework of poles, the whole overlaid with cattails. It is without doubt the best duck blind I ever saw anywhere, and I built it to introduce you, at last, to the sport of duck shooting."

"Some other time," I concluded.

"I'm afraid," said Jim, "you are a fair-weather sport. You miss the true essence and spirit of sport. Sport involves all the manlier human attributes, such as taking risks and overcoming danger. The true sportsman fares forth in the face of the elements and by his own devices outwits the elements. That is why duck shooting is the premier sport of all. It calls upon a sportsman's resources to keep dry and warm. You can't hunt ducks on a fine warm day. You've got to be in the blinds before dawn, and the worse the weather the better will the ducks fly."

"It sounds as horrible as ever," I informed him.

"To me," cried Jim, "it's the greatest thrill in the world. We get up at 4 a.m. It is still pitch dark and the wind is sighing over the farmhouse. We dress by lamplight, gradually coming back to consciousness. Minute by minute, our sense of appreciation of life seems to grow sharper. We put on our heavy clothes, our canvas coats and our wind and rainproof covers.

"I love bed," I gloated, "Deep, tumbly bed."

Those Rushing Targets

"We go out into the air," went on Jim, "and it is dark and strange and tingling and sharp. The blood leaps. Stars shine coldly. We have our guns across our bent arms, and what a queer lovely feeling that is. Our pockets bulge with boxes of shells."

"I'm still in bed," I said. "Yah, I stretch my legs down under the quilts."

"We walk down across the dark fields," said Jim, "to where the punt is tied on the edge of the bog, and there it is, looming, with its pile of decoys all ready in the middle. Silently, our heavy boots crunching in the frosty rim of the water's edge, we get in and push off. We pole and paddle amidst pale ghostly aisles of bog, listening every now and then to the sleepy quack of ducks or to the faint whistle of wings of ducks already stirring. We hurry. We reach the point of bog, putting into the dark, windy water, where we quickly toss out our decoys, draw the punt deep into the rushes to hide it, and fumble our way into the waiting blind."

"I fumble the quilts up higher about my head," I put in.

"We unload our pockets," continued Jim. "We lay the shell boxes handy, emptying a few into our pockets, and load our guns. We button up our collars and pull our caps low. We are ready."

"And I," I said, "mutter drowsily in my sleep. Something about the chief end of man."

"All about us," sang Jimmie, "something seems stirring. There is a faint paleness. The wind freshens. Afar off we hear the muffled thud, thud of a gun. Something unseen whistles and fades overhead, a flight of ducks. Dimly the outlines of bog and shoreline begin to be visible, and we sit, crouching, gun at the ready, peering into the air. It is the dawn. It is like a symphony. It is a great, primeval thing, in vast simple tones of gray and of darkness, of sound and silence, of stirring and of motionlessness. We can now see, like little bobbing phantoms, our decoys on the water fifteen yards ahead of us. A mile to our left there is a sudden blaze of guns, two, three guns, blasting in quick succession. We tense. We crouch and take a fresh grip of our guns."

"Go on," I said.

"There we crouch," said Jimmie. "And then faintly, faintly to our ears comes a hissing, indescribable sound, increasing like the rush of arrows through the air. Through the peep-holes we have left in the cattails of our blind we suddenly see, like shadows, far beyond our decoys, a close packed flock of ducks curving through the air. They have seen our decoys. They lift and turn. Our pulses are beating like hammers. Our breath nearly stops. With a rush of sound they come, like arrows slackening in their flight, straight into our decoys. Ten feet above the decoys they bend their wings to brake their speed, and in a kind of innocent jumble prepare to drop down among the wooden deceivers."

"Go on," I said.

"We rise," said Jim. "All in one smooth motion, we rise to our feet and aim our guns. Bang, bang, bang, we pick our birds and drop them. The others, suddenly towering, try to make off, with loud quacks of fright. We swing and follow with our gun barrels, in that eerie light, the flashes showing us we aimed too far ahead or not enough, and a couple more of those rushing targets fall to the water."

"How many did we get?" I asked.

"Six," said Jim. "Three each."

"Oh, boy," I said, because a roast wild duck, served with wild rice, creamed celery and apple sauce, is just about as nice a thing as ever a man got out of bed for.

"We hurriedly push the punt out of the rushes," said Jim, "and pick up our kill. Then we hide the punt as quickly again and crouch down in the blind."

So that was how I was betrayed by Jimmie into going duck shooting. To my outfit for normal sport I added canvas coats and hip rubber boots, which are good for nothing but washing a car. Firemen wear them, but firemen don't have to walk in them. They ride.

We arrived at the farmhouse about 9 p.m., but the good woman insisted on feeding us, and there was potted meat and pies made out of greenings, so it was eleven o'clock before we finally got into the spare bed, which was hard and cold. And I don't believe I got my eyes really shut before I found Jim with the lamp lit shaking me roughly and telling me to get up.

It was not only dark and cold, but a wind that I identified as an east wind was sighing and moaning around the side of the farmhouse. Canvas was never intended to be worn. It is for tents and horse covers. We pulled on our clammy underwear and our canvas and our high rubber boots. We gathered up guns and shell boxes with clumsy hands. I ached all over for sleep. That bed fairly held out its arms to me. But shivering and hoarsely whispering, we stood forth and Jim blew out the lamp.

"Rain," I said, as we opened the door and stepped out.

"A swell morning," said Jim with hoarse enthusiasm. "A perfect morning. And not a smell of rain."

"East wind," I shuddered, "always brings rain. Just a minute."

I had seen an umbrella hanging on a nail the night before. I slipped back in and fumbled for it. I took it down and rolled it, with my gun in the rubber sheet I was taking along to sit on in the blind.

Down the yard and out across the pasture we walked, in the complete darkness, no stars glittering however coldly, and heavy clods sticking up to further impede the loose and hollowly clumping, rubber boots. We found the punt, and as Jim had foretold there loomed the pile of decoys in the middle of it.

I clamped down in the bow while Jim, with a long oar, poled and paddled us across the windy little bays of the bog. It took us fifteen minutes to get out to the point where Jimmie had made his blind the week before. As we neared it a voice, muffled and low in the dark, called out:

"Hey, on your way. This is occupied."

Jim stopped poling and let the punt drift nearer.

"Beat it," came the voice. "Make it snappy."

"Look here," said Jim, "I built this blind."

"Go on," said the voice—it sounded like a large, rough sort of person, "beat it. We build our blind on this point every year."

"You're in my blind," stated Jim sharply.

"So what?" said the voice, and faintly I could now make out two massive figures looming head and shoulders out of what seemed a mass of wet and cold swamp.

With an angry shove, Jim pushed away and started paddling past. I could see decoys on the dark water.

"The dirty crooks," said Jim bitterly.

"Let's go back," I said, "to the farmhouse."

"There's lots more good spots," said Jim. "In fact, one of the best spots of all is only a quarter mile out here."

I slunk down lower. The east wind was rising. There was a horrible ghastly paleness seeming to grow all about. Jim paddled furiously with the oar, standing up, and the wet little punt wobbled and teetered across the leaden water, the small busy waves making a most unpleasant sound along the sides.

"Take it easy, Jim," I suggested.

We drew on towards a point of bog jutting out darkly. As we approched a sharp whistle rang across the murk.

"Hey," a voice called. "Full up here."

Jim swung the punt and headed furiously in a new direction. It was paling. Far off, I heard a faint double thud of a gun being fired. Jim made the punt wobble dangerously as he drove the oar into the water.

"If we dumped here—" I began.

But Jim just made an extra wild wobble that cut me short. We hove off another point of bog. A dog barked at us. A voice called angrily words that we could not hear.

From the point where Jim had built his blind came the sharp bang of two pump-guns firing furiously.

"It's begun," said Jim, swinging the punt out and resting his oar.

Every Man To His Taste

And it had begun. The paleness had increased until now, dimly, we could see the shoreline. The wind had freshened. On the edge of our limit of vision we saw a flock of ducks, flying low and fast, streak along, and a moment later a fusillade of shots broke from another point. Far off and near at hand, the firing swelled.

"We'll just push in here anywhere," said Jim excitedly.

He headed for the cattail bog and, on nearing it, commanded me sharply to set out the decoys while he held the punt steady. The decoys were cold and icy. They each had a string with a lead weight for an anchor. The strings were tangled and I had to double down and peer and jerk and untangle. I laid them in the water and got my hands numb with the cold trying to make them ride right side up. There were twenty of them.

We got them set out somehow and Jim, feeling with his oar, found a soft spot in the bog where he shoved the punt in amidst the tall rushes. I having to get half out of the punt to help shove with my foot. It was cold and terribly wet and smelled of swamp.

We got set. We managed to turn the punt sideways to allow both of us a shot if any ducks did come in to our decoys.

But no duck did come. We sat there, listening to the far-off cannonade and the sudden fury of the guns nearby. Far off, as the day dawned, we beheld harried flights of ducks crossing ever farther out and ever higher.

It became broad gray daylight, the east wind was now a mild gale and there came the first sprinkle of small, drifting rain.

"Well," I inquired bitterly, "now what do we do?"

The firing had died down. Desultory shots sounded on the wind in the rushes.

"I guess we can go back now," said Jim dully.

So while Jim held the punt steady in the lashing wind, I picked the decoys up.

"Wind the strings around each one," said Jim, "so they won't get all tangled."

The water was icy. It ran down my wrists. My hands were no longer gifted with any feeling. They were red and raw looking.

As we started to push away from the bog to cross the homeward bay the rain began to thicken. I reached down and unwrapped the umbrella from the rubber sheet. I shook it out and sprung it open.

"What on earth have you got there?" demanded Jimmie, as if he couldn't see.

"It's an umbrella," I explained. "A device invented some hundreds of years ago by the Chinese to add to the comfort of human kind."

I heard a whisking sound.

"Hye!" roared Jim, and the punt gave a sickening wobble.

A big fat mallard had jumped from the bog behind us and nearly collided with my umbrella.

"We couldn't have got off a shot in time anyway," I stated.

"I guess," said Jim thinly, "I guess it's best not to try to interest people in duck shooting. Either you've got it in you or you haven't got it in you. You're born to shoot ducks, I guess."

"Every man to his taste," I agreed.

So I kept the umbrella up all the way across to the farm and all the way up to the house, where we had a great breakfast of eggs, ham, apple sauce, potted meat, apple pie made of greenings, thick toast made over a wood fire and boiled tea.

"I leaned forward and dropped the puck
. . . it was as if lightning had struck the
place."

Hurray For Our Side

February 5, 1938

"Well," said Jimmie Frise, "I guess we're snowed up."

"Nonsense, Jimmie," I heartened him, "let's get that farmer in there to tow us through this drift. Maybe this is the last drift between here and Toronto."

"Look," expostulated Jim, "we've spent four dollars already on being towed out of four drifts. The nearer we get to Toronto, the higher goes the price of being towed out of drifts. What we've got to do is settle down somewhere for the night and wait for the snowplows to clear the highways."

"Aw," I protested, "I hate spending the night in a strange farm house, ousting some poor hired man out of his rightful bed."

"Farmhouse be hanged," cried Jim, "we'll get this farmer here to haul the car into his lane and we'll leave it there. Then we'll get him to drive us in a cutter to the nearest town. There's a light in the distance, see?"

It had just turned dark, and through the murk and

mighty swirl of the blizzard, we could dimly see the tops of fence posts, the shadowy form of a line of evergreens marking the lane of an old-fashioned farm house, and far down the lonely and swiftly drifting road, the faint glare of headlights of cars stalled like ourselves, and beyond them the fainter suspicion of the lights of a town.

"Jim," I stated, "this is a lesson to us to read the probabilities before we set out on long motor trips in the winter."

"I did read them," assured Jim, "and they said fair and mild."

"I hate," I stated, "spending the night in some strange little town. In the first place, hotels have gone out of the hotel business all over the country. They're either just big boarding houses, where local garage men and Hydro linesmen put up. Or else, after passing from hand to hand downwards in an ever-weakening decline, they are now in the possession of some still hopeful old hotelman who lives there with two of his daughters and seven grandchildren, and nothing in the world staggers and upsets them more than to have guests arrive."

"Don't you believe it," said Jim, as we sat there in the warm car firmly sunk and imbedded in a big curving snowdrift, "there are some mighty pleasant little hotels in some of these small towns."

"With Bible texts hung around the walls," said I.

"The tourist traffic," corrected Jim, "has revived some of these small town hotels in the last few years. I've been in some dandies."

"The beds," I muttered, "cold and damp. The bacon a quarter of an inch thick. And the eggs—leathery. And mashed potatoes served with the bacon and eggs for breakfast. Ugh! A side dish of slightly browned and slightly warmed mashed potatoes."

"I guess our troubles of the past two hours," said Jim, kindly, "have got you down."

"Why did we ever start for home?" I cried.

"Because you insisted," retorted Jim.

"Well, why did you give in?" I triumphed angrily.

"Let's go in and see if this farmer will tow us off the road and gives us a cutter ride to town," said Jim.

Not So Dull

We got out of the car, leaving the headlights glaring, and waded and hopped heavily through the great edge-crested drifts towards the long line of firs at the far end of which glowed home lights. And we found the household just finishing dinner in the great old kitchen, the room at about 100 degrees Fahrenheit from the immense stove, the table stacked so high with provender, the one side of the table could hardly see the other. They invited us to stop for supper, which we did, having hot roast pork, cold head cheese and cold ham, mashed potatoes, and sliced turnips and carrots mixed, a most delightful combination, sliced in long, thin fingers. The bread was home made, the apple sauce was spiced with cloves and there were cookies made of oatmeal with dates in them that I wish you could have tasted. Around this table, watching Jimmie and me eat, were the elderly father and mother, two middle-aged daughters and two middle-aged sons and one child of eight. Their whole interest in life, outside of turning on the news broadcast so loud that it shook all the shelves of the kitchen, was to see us eat. They passed and handed and urged and shoved. They high-pressured and ganged up on us.

And after we had eaten, and they had turned off the radio the minute the raucous newscast was ended, we all went into the next room, ladies and all, where one of the men sat at the piano and we all sang Harry Lauder songs while he chorded more or less accurately. To feed to suffocation and to sing as loud as possible was the ritual of entertainment in this grand old Ontario home, with all of them acting as if we were nightly guests in their midst. And then, reluctantly, one of the men said:

"Well, gents, if we're going to town we'd better go now, because the game is at 8 o'clock sharp."

"Game?" said Jimmie.

"Hockey game," said Ed, which was his name. "The junior finals for this district."

"Man," cried Jim, "my friend here has been complaining about having to spend the night in some dull little town."

113

"He'll not be complaining," laughed Ed, taking his coat off the door. "It's our town against Buckleton, only twenty miles west. That makes for friendly rivalry."

"If they ever get here," I suggested.

"They'd get here," said Ed, "if they had to climb the Rocky Mountains. They figure on beating us on our own ice."

Everybody laughed and Jim said, "what a hope."

And in a few minutes we had the car towed off the highway into the lane and an old-fashioned farm sleigh hitched with two horses, laden with hay and bedded with robes, quilts and blankets, into and under which we all got, including the old and the young; and with bells jangling mellowly we drove out the tall firred lane and on to the highway.

What had been a blizzard, an enemy, frustrating and menacing to us in our modern high-power car, was now a thing of beauty, the great wind and the dry snow sweeping and driving helplessly over us, while we in our sleigh conquered. The deepest drifts which to modernity had been impassable, the two hearty horses simply went around or plunged straight through. We slewed and tipped and swung, but all was merry and chattery, and Ed and his brother, hunched in their old brown fur coats on the driving seat above us, kept up a strong sound to the horses, the bells grew to a music chimed to the white and lovely night; and, when one of the women started sweetly to sing "Blessed Be the Tie That Binds," and we all softly joined, I do not think in all my life anything so suddenly and simply filled me with the sense of beauty. I thought of the poor, silly world, striving with its little machines to master, and only being mastered; a thousand million monkeys on a thousand million sticks.

We came in twenty minutes to the town, and down its main street with cars angle-parked and half buried before the steamy windowed shops. The streets were busy with bent and side-ways figures thrusting into the blizzard, all heading one way. The game.

We drove into a great yard and the horses were unhitched and led into a shed. Through the snow we walked out to the street and to a large domed rink, a simple great curve of roof. Through unpainted entrances and halls, ice cold, we filed and so to the rink. Inside, on rough narrow benches, the great throng was already gathered, the rink was full of loud noise, yells and echoing cries. We were crowded into seats, but all around us were packed the bright country people, with their eager or quiet faces, the shy girls who stared stonily in front, and the girls not shy who, twisting and turning their heads to look up at the ranks behind and above them, were full of nudges and ducks and laughs and giggles. Small towns are full of girlish intrigue.

Where we sat with our new-found friends was in the midst of the home-town section. Across from us, a section not so full yet, had been reserved for the Buckleton rooters.

"I Can't Skate"

The rink continued to fill until it seemed it could hold no more. Suddenly, amidst a great hosanna, the home team started to stumble out on to the ice and then the Buckleton team followed and the din became deafening. Ed, who had been down at the rail talking to some of the players, came back up with a look of anxiety on him.

"The referee isn't here yet," he said. "And the managers won't agree on any local man, either here or in the Buckleton crowd."

"Referee?" cried Jimmie. "Why, Ed, you've got a referee right here."

"Who?" said Ed and I together.

"Why, Mr. Clark," cried Jim excitedly. "Did you ever hear of the West Toronto Juniors?"

"Did I?" cried Ed, looking at me with wonder.

"Well, Mr. Clark," said Jim, "was a member of the executive of the West Toronto Juniors. They were O.H.A. champions in 1931. They were runners-up in 1932."

I just sat and smiled comfortably.

"Mr. Clark," cried Ed, "would you referee?"

"No, no, no," I exclaimed. "No, no, no."

"Of course he will," shouted Jimmie standing up. "Certainly he will. He's only shy. Come on, go down, Ed, and ask the teams if a member of the West Toronto club will

115

do for referee."

"No, no, Ed, no, no," I shouted, rising, and trying to catch Ed as he floundered down through the crowded benches. I saw him, as in a daze, beckoning to players and a group gathering. I saw interested, almost reverent gazes lifted to me. I sat down weakly.

"Come on," said Jim. "Get out to the dressing room. We can borrow skates."

"Jim, Jim," I begged, "I don't know anything about hockey. I was just on the executive to get the team some publicity and wangle radio announcements."

"Come on," commanded Jim, starting to shove me. "You can referee a game. Just ring the bell every now and then and face off."

"But, Jim," I gasped, struggling to sit down, "I don't even know an off-side. I never did know an off-side. I've sat through hundreds of games . . ."

"Just ring the bell," said Jim, who had hoisted me up and started shoving me past everybody's knees. The teams were now ganged up below, looking very happy about the whole thing, and a voice in a megaphone was explaining. I heard my name. I heard West Toronto Juniors. I heard loud roars and boos.

All perspiring and dazzled, I was led down icy cold alleys to a dressing room, where a half a dozen managers were introduced and somebody had me sitting down sizing me up for skates.

"Jim," I said, bending him near, "listen, I can't even skate. I haven't been on skates for thirty years."

"Aw, anybody can skate," said Jim.

"Jim, listen," I begged. "I tell you, I never really took any interest in hockey. I was only a member of the committee to help wangle things. Look: I don't know the rules."

"Ring your bell," said Jim. "That's all there is to it."

"Jim, you don't understand," I cried, "all the years I went to hockey games I wasn't following the play, I was watching some one guy, the goalie or a defence man or even some funny looking bird in the crowd. I tell you I can't go on with this. I don't know the first rule . . ."

"Do you realize," hissed Jim, "that you are holding up

a great crowd that will be bitterly disappointed if the game is called? And if you won't serve. . ."

They arrived with skates. They brought a rather over-size white sweater for me. I took off my coat and put on the skates with numb and trembling fingers. It was all blurry and confused, it was like that dream of the house on fire.

"Have you a copy of the rules?" I demanded, standing up.

"Yes, sir," cried one of the Buckleton management, handing me a little frayed book from his pocket. I pretended to study up a paragraph or two. I had never seen the book before in my life, except in Doc MacIntyre's hand.

Amidst the sense of hurry, I started out the alleys, accompanied by a respectful and helpful throng of managers and coaches, Jimmie helping me from behind.

The ice was icy. Amidst deep cheers I stepped down on to it, clinging to the rail. I was handed the bell and I rang it authoritatively, after the fashion I had seen scores of junior hockey referees waggle it. I stepped forth and slid for the centre of the ice, in the pot-bellied, ponderous way referees do, reflecting dimly the while that, after all, most hockey referees are punk skaters. I hoped my initial shove from the rail would carry me to the middle.

It did. I came to a slow, dignified stop, just exactly about middle ice, and once again I waggled the bell and stood ready. Amidst a deepening stillness, the teams took up their positions, and the two centre men skated towards me. The home town boy was an enormous lad for eighteen. He was red-headed, rugged and ugly. He looked about twenty-four to me. The Buckleton centre was a long, lean youth with a very wicked expression on his face for one so young, according to the rules.

Glancing around at the players, in the way I had seen referees do, I leaned forward and dropped the puck.

Calling 'Em Wrong

It was as if lightning had struck the place. A sudden rocketing roar filled the rink, the two figures before me

117

slashed and leaped and from all sides flying figures seemed to come in blazing colors and at inhuman speed, while I stood paralyzed. Things in general seemed to be moving towards one end of the ice, so cautiously I followed. A thunderclap of sound suddenly exploded amidst the deafening roar; I saw a red light blink on down there where I was heading and those solid cliffs of human flesh on all sides seemed to be lifted by pandemonium, they became a living storm of humanity, leaping, waving, and roaring.

"Good," I muttered, "A goal. Now I just skate back to the middle again."

But to me, in vast furious curves, came figures blazing and surrounded me, all shouting, glaring, waving immense gauntletted hands and arms. I pushed resolutely through the gathering cluster, and picked the puck up out of the net, where a goalie lay, face down as if dead. I picked the puck up and started to skate back to centre ice.

It was all over very suddenly. The sound, which had been continuous, and filling the air like wool, all on the instant seemed to double and throb and vibrate. It was a formidable sound. I was instantly surrounded by multi-colored players, who started shoving me and thrusting and I could see the infuriated face of the red-headed centre man bent low down, his eyes rolling . . . Through the gaps in this milling mob I could see things being thrown on the ice, and one glimpse I got of Jimmie, standing down at the rail, leaning forward, his familiar face purple and . . . booing!

Yes, booing. I felt the impact of something striking the outer rim of the mob around me, which, by its colors, I took to be the members of the Buckleton team, and then the lights went out.

Something crashed into me and I went down under a heap of fighting, grunting bodies, the din grew high with screams, and I covered my face and head with my arms, saying "so this is hockey."

I heard a low voice near me grating my name.

"Jim," I replied wildly, "Jim."

It was Jim. And he dragged me **across** the darkness of

ice and hoisted me over the rail. Through unseen and fighting shapes, he propelled me between rough plank walls to what, when the lights came on, proved to be the dressing room where my dear old overcoat lay, friendly.

"You booed," I yelled.

"The goal was off-side," shouted Jim back. "Miles off-side. And you allowed it."

"A good referee," I shouted, "always calls 'em as he sees 'em. I've heard Lou Marsh say that."

"Yeah," retorted Jim, "but not on home ice. That was the Buckleton team shoved that one in."

So the game was called on account of the unavoidable absence of the referee.

Style Is
Everything

April 30, 1938

"I had one real lunker on, but he took my fly," said Jimmie. I said nothing, pretending not to be conscious of the fish on the log . . .

"The moths," declared Jimmie Frise, "have got into my trout flies."

"Hhmmff," I laughed.

"Yeah," cried Jim, "a lot of sympathy I get from you. You who have 3,000 trout flies and me with my poor little two or three dozen all eaten and frazzled by moths."

"Don't expect," I warned him, "to bum any trout flies off me, my boy. The reason I have such a wonderful collection of trout flies is that I care for them. I keep them. I don't let the moths get 'em and I don't give them away to half-hearted anglers who look on fishing as if it were a sideline."

"A sideline?" inquired Jim. "How do you mean sideline?"

"Angling," I informed him eloquently, "is an art, not a mere recreation. It is an art, just as much as painting, sculpture or music. It is one of the oldest arts, because we find writings on fly fishing amongst the ancient Greeks and Romans. It is an art that has been practised and developed through the centuries, accompanied all the way by an ever-increasing wealth of beautiful literature, poetry and prose."

"Phoo," said Jim; "all I started to say was the moths got into my trout flies. And here you go making a public speech."

"It serves you right, the moths," I stated. "Where did you store your fly book over the winter?"

"I didn't store it," said Jim. "I just popped it in a drawer in a sort of carpenter's bench in the garage."

"Ah," I mused, "just popped it? The season being over last summer, you showed your gratitude to all those delightful little confections, for the sport they had given you, by just popping them. I tell you, when the fishing season ends I spend night after night sorting and rearranging my trout flies. I get them carefully arranged. I then prepare a big tin can, with a friction top, such a can as wholesale candies come in, a can almost as big as a bushel basket. I line its rim with adhesive tape. I spread a dozen moth balls on the bottom. Then I place my fly books and boxes reverently within, for their winter sleep. It is a ceremony. Such a ceremony as Wotan staged when he set his daughter, Brunhilde, asleep on a mountain top, with the magic fire burning around her to guard her."

"Mmmf, mfff, mfff," said Jimmie.

"In fact, this coming autumn," I declared, "I believe I will get a phonograph record of the Fire Music from Die Walkure and play it the night I am setting my trout flies away for the winter. It would be the fitting thing to do."

"Ho, ho, hum," stretched Jimmie. "I'll be glad to be fishing."

The Ceremonial of Fishing

"Jim," I informed him, "you don't get half the pleasure out of fishing you should. You don't invest fishing with any imagination, any ceremony. You should dramatize it. All you get out of fishing is a trip into the country, a day spent in pleasant idleness and a few fish."

"What more do I want?" inquired Jim.

"My dear man," I protested, "if you could only realize the pleasure I get out of the ceremonial of fishing. The gear. The perfection of equipment. The garb. The dressing up and equipping of myself with Scotch waders, with short fishing jacket replete with pockets; with ingenious places for all my fly boxes, my scissors and gut cutters, my priest or fish killer; my weigh scales, my water thermometer, for testing the temperature of the stream before fishing; my oil bottle for dry flies, my measuring rule, my spear, in case I want to attach it to the butt of the rod to spike it into the earth while I pause to rest at the pool."

"I've seen you," submitted Jim. "You look like a fishing tackle show-case on casters."

"Is that so?" I inquired. "Might I ask if you have inspected your rod lately?"

"It doesn't need inspection," said Jim, "it was in good shape last season."

"Where is it?" I demanded.

Jim did some thinking.

"It's in my den," he said.

"Whereabouts?"

"Standing up."

"Standing up where?" I insisted.

"Behind the radiator," said Jim. "In the corner."

I shuddered aloud.

"And your fly line?" I inquired. "I suppose it has been on the reel all winter?"

"It's in the drawer," said Jim, "in the garage, with my fly book."

"Jim," I pleaded, "don't you know, that a fly line will go all tacky and sticky if you leave it on the reel? Do you know how I keep my lines? At the close of the season I take them off the reels, wipe them most carefully, and put them in a box, bedded deep in a powder consisting of Fuller's earth and pure talc?"

"Sure, sure," said Jim. "And haven't you got some kind of a steel vault in your cellar, with time locks on it, to keep your reels in?"

"Aw, Jim," I said, "what shape will your gear be in when we arrive at the trout stream?"

"It'll be O.K.," said Jim, firmly. "My rubber boots had a couple of leaks, but I patched them up for the duck season last fall and they're fine."

"Very well." I stated clearly. "But don't expect to outfit yourself from my supply of flies and leaders when we arrive up there. Don't figure I'm in the tackle business, with goods to sell to improvident anglers at the waterside . . ."

"Did I ever?" demanded Jim.

"No, but you always look to me as if you ought to," I explained.

Highest Moment

And with this understanding we passed on into more agreeable discussion of the impending trout season. It is a wide question whether the actual fishing season or the closed season gives fishermen the most pleasure.

We arrived on the eve of opening day at our dear and

accustomed trout stream. We arrived in plenty of time to take a walk up the banks of the little river so as to see what the past winter had done to it, with freshets; what old logs had been swept away and what new logs had come; what pools were deeper and what pools were more filled up with silt. And we spent a most happy hour, with darkness creeping reluctantly down, and all the new birds singing amidst the barren underbrush and leafless woods, because spring is tardy where the best fishing is.

And at daybreak, from the farmhouse where we stay on these visits, we set out after a lamplit breakfast of two eggs and thick country bacon and toast made of that homemade bread that is high and holey over the glowing coals of a hardwood fire.

In the dawn Jim looked particularly dilapidated. He had on an old hat that had been white felt. His shirt was a bright scarlet, a hunting shirt. His waders sagged about his legs in a curiously elephantine way.

"Jim," I protested, "that hat and that shirt will scare all the trout out of the river."

"They were all right last season," said Jim.

"To get fish," I stated, "your clothes should be gray and brown, obscure tones to blend with the underbrush of the streamside."

"These are O.K.," said Jim, producing from his hip pocket a tin cigarette box, which he opened and pawed about amidst the contents, finally extracting a leader which, in the half light, I could see was twisted, milky in color and generally unsuited for fishing; and to it was tied a ragged, colorless fly that had been left on it all winter.

"Didn't you damp your leader?" I cried.

"Let's go fishing," said Jim. And we started down for the stream.

At the streamside we stood and rigged our rods. That is perhaps the highest moment of the fisherman's year, the rigging of the rod on the first morning of the season. In the pearly light the stream, beloved and familiar, runs with a laughing sound of welcome. It seems actually to be greeting you. Your hands tremble with excitement as you joint up the rod, fasten on the reel and thread up the line through the guides. Jim, in jointing up his rod, pulled one of the ferrules right off the wood.

"Have you got any ferrule cement, by any chance, amongst all your junk?" inquired he.

"If I had," I retorted, "I doubt if I would lend it to you."

So Jim hunted around and selected a sliver of grass which he wedged in and forced the ferrule to stick in place.

"There you are," he said, waving the rod back and forth. It gave out a clicking sound. Every ferrule was loose.

I cut my rod through the air, making a smooth, whooshing sound, perfect, beautiful.

As Jim started to peel the line off his reel, I could hear the small sticky sound of the oil-impregnated line protesting.

"Ha, line ruined?" I said pleasantly.

"Just dandy," said Jim, threading it up. And while I bent onto the end of my line a nine-foot gut cast tapered to three X, fresh out of my damper box, Jim proceeded to knot on to his the coiled, springy, milk-white leader with the shapeless fly which had lain all winter in the tin cigarette box Jim uses as a general receptacle for all his outfit.

"She damps up in no time, in the water," said Jim. "How will we divide? You fish up from here and I down, or vice versa?"

"It doesn't matter to me," I informed him generously.

"I'll fish right here," said Jim; "one place is as good as another."

"Jim," I said, relenting, "here, take a few flies. Let me give you this Rogue, and these March Browns, with the red underwing . . ."

"Pshaw, no," said Jim. "I've got five or six flies in my hat."

And in his hat he had, from last season, a few brittle, faded-looking little squibs of feather, nondescript and hopeless.

"Jim," I said, selecting three or four of my favorite

125

patterns, "here, my boy."

"I'll use them if I run short," said Jim, sticking them carelessly in his hat, a horrible custom.

I left him, staggering heavily in his clumsy and patched rubber boots down into the margin of the pool. It is not a good pool. It just happens to be the handiest pool on your way down from the farmhouse, and all the lazy men fish it. I have known Jim to spend a whole evening of June, with trout rising madly up and down as far as you can see, absurdly anchored at this one spot, thrashing the water.

Pool by pool and bend by bend, I revisited the beautiful and sweet-remembered little river. The first visit to a trout stream in spring is not so much a meat-getting expedition, as I explained to Jim later, as it is a sentimental journey. How can a man, with a true understanding of the sport of angling, attend to the intricate business of casting fine and far off, when his eyes are blinded with the beauty of old scenes and his mind distracted by a hundred memories of bygone battles, victories and losses? I spent four blessed hours on the upper end of the stream. I cast as well as a man should, at the first of the season. I got two good rises, both of which I missed due to over-eagerness; and I caught three small trout which were below the limit and had to be returned unharmed to the water. I sat down at certain spots more sacred than others and spent a little time in happy contemplation. And when the dinner gong made of an iron rail rang sweetly across the fields from the farmhouse, I wended my way down to pick up Jimmie.

Terrible Technique

He had not moved. He was sitting on a log, in his bright shirt and dirty white hat, and his clumsy hip boots now fallen around his ankles, a picture of complete and soaking dilapidation. He was tying a fresh fly on to a remnant of his rotted leader, 18 inches long. It was not even one of my good flies. It was one of the remaining brittle and shapeless things he had worn in his hat for goodness knows how many seasons past.

And his rod had smashed somewhere short of the top joint and had been repaired with string. I stood back and surveyed him unseen.

"What a figure," I called, startling him, "of an angler!"

"What luck?" he called back cheerfully

"Two good rises and three or four little ones I didn't keep," I informed him. "But a glorious morning."

I'll be with you," he said, "in just one jiffy. I want one more cast in here."

I advanced.

"Jim," I offered heartily, "here, try my rod."

"Oh, this'll do," he replied.

And then I saw, on the log, laid out in splendor, such a mess of trout as you seldom see outside of paintings.

Jewelled, gleaming, bluish, olive, speckled with scarlet and metallic blue, their milk-white fins margined with orange . . .

"I had one real lunker on," said Jim, musing, "But he took my fly."

I said nothing. I sat down on the log in the place he had vacated. I sat there, watching him thrash the pool as if he were fly swatting instead of fly fishing. I pretended not to be conscious of my jewelled companions on the log.

Jim made a specially tangled and confused cast, the line flopping noisily on to the water. There was a hump and a boil.

"Gottim," roared Jim; staggering and floundering backward furiously out of the pool, and dragging the loveliest trout you ever saw flapping on to the bank.

"My net," gasped Jim, "broke on the first one."

"Where's your creel?" I inquired stiffly, rising.

"I'll just carry them on a forked stick," said Jim, walking up with the newest and largest writhing in his grip.

"I'll carry them in my creel," I offered, magnanimously.

"No," said Jim, "I'll just carry them on a forked stick."

Over the Yardarm

May 7, 1938

*"I think you'd better change the paint," said the stranger. "That red looks like a political declaration."
"Is that so?" said Jim.*

"Talk about bargains," cried Jimmie Frise, excitedly, "have I ever got one!"

"Nobody ever really gets a bargain, Jim," I assured him. "The last one I got had scored cylinders, its axle was bent, it had fleas in its upholstery and it back-fired."

"This is a boat," said Jim breathlessly. "Oh, boy, a sloop."

"A boat," I informed him, "is never a bargain. Probably the wood in it is all punky. Probably it is top heavy or something."

"I've got its record," chattered Jim, "it was in a bunch of races only last season. It nearly won some of them."

"A boat," I informed him, "is never cheap."

"It's a sloop," described Jim, "the dream of my life. Twenty-six foot hull, with two sails, a mains'l and a jib."

"I see," I said. "One of those things you always have to invite a gang on, to help pull ropes and yo heave ho."

"A sloop, imagine," sighed Jim. "The loveliest stream-lined thing you ever saw. With a little cabin that will easily sleep four, forrard."

"Don't expect me," I said, "to spend all my weekends this summer going out blistering around the lake with you."

"Guess," said Jim, standing up with excitement, "guess how much I paid for it? A sloop."

"Five bucks? Ten bucks?" I said bitterly.

"Fifty bucks," shouted Jim terrifically. "Fifty bucks. For a sloop. A sloop. A new sloop costs $1,500. I know guys have spent $500 for a second-hand one."

"You must have got a dandy for $50," I consoled him.

"I've just come," gasped Jimmie, sitting down again, "from seeing it. I can hardly believe it."

"You can't get me excited about any boats." I assured him.

"Wait till you see her," pleaded Jim. "Honestly, I can hardly contain myself. This fellow called me last night. Mr. Frise, he said, I've been an admirer of your cartoons for many years, he said. Mr. Frise, are you interested in sailing? And I said yes."

"I never knew you were interested in sailing?" I informed him.

"Well, I am," stated Jim. "Before the war, I had a dinghy down on Toronto Bay. I used to sail a lot. But I never dreamed I could ever afford a yacht."

"A yacht?" I inquired.

"Sure it's a yacht," declared Jim. "Within the meaning of the term yachting. You go yachting, see? This is a sloop. Can't you see it? Twenty-six feet long, eight-foot beam."

"So you're in the Vanderbilt class at last," I submitted.

"I want you to come home along the Lake Shore with me," said Jim earnestly, "and have a look at it. It's the strangest thing. Fifty bucks."

"It can't be any good, Jim," I reasoned with him.

A Secret Dream

"It's like this," said Jim. "This fellow who likes my cartoons has been transferred by his firm out west to Regina. There is no sailing out there. So he just said to himself, look, he says, I've had my money's worth out of the Minnie, he says. That's her name. Why should I waste time hustling around trying to sell her? I'll never get what she's worth anyway, he said to himself. So what did he do? He just sat there trying to think of somebody he would like to have her. Like finding a good home for a dog you love. It's the same thing, really."

"You're all flushed, Jim," I advised him.

"So would you be," cried Jim, "if a secret dream of yours suddenly came true."

"She may have wood beetles in her hull or something," I muttered.

"I've just come from seeing her, I tell you," said Jim. "And I could hardly believe my eyes. There she was. I spoke to an old caretaker at a boathouse nearby and he showed me her sails in his loft. They're fresh and new and not even a spot of mildew."

"It certainly doesn't make sense," I admitted. "My brother got a sail for his boy's dinghy last summer and it alone cost $75."

"It's just one of those things," said Jim, "that happen to a man now and then to make up for all the bad breaks."

So on the way home for supper we went down by the

Lake Shore Rd., and Jim drove me down on to a sandy path that led to the beach where large numbers of boats of all kinds, launches, cruisers, sailing craft of every description, were either hauled up on skids or partly launched or in the water at anchor. Several men in shabby overalls and yachting caps were to be seen, pipe in mouth, busily painting, scraping or pottering around different boats. It is the overhaul season.

Jim leaped out of the car and led me eagerly over the sand to a separate row where about a dozen small craft, mostly sloops, were sitting up on their winter scaffolding.

"There she is," said Jim in a low, passionate voice. "Second from the end."

"Boy," I breathed.

And Jim stepped proudly forward and patted the little sloop's nose tenderly.

In a moment, we were swarming aboard her. She was lovely. Trim, tidy, hardly a crack or a wrinkle.

"Some real sailor," I admitted, "owned this baby."

"Her former skipper," said Jim, leaning nautically with crossed ankles, "was certainly a sailor. He told me she was light as a feather to handle, rode like a gull on the water, steady as a rock."

"Boy," I said, exploring down into the little cabin, forrard. "A man wouldn't really get blistered much, on a weekend, if he could lie in here most of the time. Where are you going to sail her, Skipper?"

"I'm going to spend every weekend, from Saturday noon to Monday morning, cruising," stated Jim, coming in and sitting down in the dinky little cabin with me. "I'm going to explore up and down both shores of Lake Ontario. I'm going to study charts and navigation. Maybe next year, I'll take a cruise down the St. Lawrence or maybe into the upper lakes."

"Jim," I said, "isn't there something cosy about the little cabin of a sailing craft?"

"You're telling me?" replied Jim, rakishly.

"I can understand the genius of a Nelson," I admitted, "living his life in a cabin of a ship year in and year out. A sailing ship."

"There is nothing like sail," declared Jimmie. "Sail, me lad; the history of our race is written in sail."

"I might," I suggested, "accept a couple of weekend invitations after all, Jim. I never really felt a ship before. This is a ship."

"You're welcome," announced Jim, "to come as often as you like. In fact, I was almost considering asking you if you'd like to take a half interest in her. But then, I thought you had your own interests, your fishing and summer cottage and stuff."

"Isn't it funny," I said, "that Canadians aren't a more marine-minded people? Here we have the greatest body of fresh water in the world, the Great Lakes. And all over the Dominion, thousands of lakes great and small. Yet we are content to putter around in canoes and row boats. It's amazing."

I got up and went astern and sat looking up where the mast and towering sail would be. I leaned out far to windard.

"When are you going to launch her, Jim?" I called.

"As soon as she's painted," said he. "I'm going to give her a coat of the finest white above the water line; and below, a bright cherry red. Can you see her heeling over in the breeze? Bright cherry?"

"Jim, let me help paint her? Let that be my contribution towards some pleasant summer cruises."

"I was hoping you'd say that," agreed Jim.

"Look," I offered eagerly, "let me buy the paint as a part share in her? What do you say? Whatever the paint comes to, that will be my share?"

"No," said Jim, gruffly, "no, a ship can't be run on shares. A ship has to have a master. An absolute master. I'm sorry, me lad, but you can work your passage in her by helping me paint."

"When are you going to start?" I asked.

"Start?" cried Jim. "I'm going to start tonight. The former owner is coming in tomorrow for his cheque, but he said to go ahead and take possession at once. Come on. I'm going to have a quick snack at home, buy a gallon of white and a gallon of red and set to. We've got three hours of daylight."

"Come on," I agreed. And we swarmed over the deck and dropped to the ground and after a long walk-around gaze at her, propped up in her sweeping beauty, we hurried to the car and sped off over the sand to the Lake Shore Rd. like a couple of sailors on shore leave.

After a hasty snack, Jim called for me and at the corner, while he was in the hardware store buying paint, I slipped into the gent's furnishings and was lucky to find, in my size, a trim little yachting cap.

Down to the Lake Shore we whirled and pulled across the sand. In the early evening, the number of fellow-mariners had greatly increased, and amidst the distant little rows and communities of boats on their props, moved the happy figures of men painting, caulking, or just sitting in ecstasy on the decks and cabin houses of their small ships.

"Now, me lad," commanded Jim very commanding, as we laid down the pails of paint alongside, "swarm aloft there and get to work with some white paint on the fittings, bowsprit and mast hole. I'll start with the red on the hull."

"Aw," I said, "let me at the hull too. I like slapping with a big brush. Let me do the . . ."

"Swarm aloft there," roared Jim, very startling. "Who the blazes is master of this ship?"

"If you let me . . ."

"One more word out of you, me hearty," said Jim, "and you'll hang from the yard arm. I've got this all figured out. I'm giving her one coat of red tonight. Tomorrow night, we'll give the upper hull a coat of white and then a second coat of red below the water line. You can do some of the trim aloft, with white. Get on with it."

"Aye, aye, Skipper," I responded, and took the white pail up and started on deck and the coaming.

Far along the beach, the quiet sounds of other mariners came to us. Out in the blue lake, the first early birds were already spreading their white sails to a pleasant breeze. I could hear Jim heartily slapping below at the hull as he rapidly spread the red lead paint thick and smooth. I laid the glaring white paint thin and neat along the deck coaming and the canvas decking.

133

An elderly man in a blue nautical cap strolled up and watched us for a while.

"A beautiful color, that red," he said.

"She'll look lovely when she heels over," Jim said.

"It's a little unusual," admitted the old fellow, "but still, we need some new ideas around here. Sailors are pretty conservative, mostly. I like a bit of color, myself."

He wandered off, and presently, just as I got the bowsprit half done and Jim was starting on the next side, another gentleman strolled up, with a cane and a sort of commodore look about him.

"Well, well," he said, stepping right up, "you're early, aren't you?"

"Not too early," said Jim, cheerfully, "look at those fellows out there on the lake already."

"H'm," said the newcomer. "Who picked your colors?"

"I did," said Jim, slapping away.

"I can't say I care for them," said the gent. "That red looks like a political declaration, and as for that white, it is the livid sort that shows up every bit of dirt it picks up out of the water."

"Is that so?" said Jim.

"Yes," said the stranger, pointing with his stick very politically too, for that matter. "I think you'd better change it."

A Bosun Sort of Voice

"Bit of a sailor, yourself, hey?" I inquired from the bowsprit.

"What's that?" roared the gentleman in a bosun sort of voice.

"What the heck affair is it of yours?" asked Jim, rising.

"Well, it's my boat, isn't it?" demanded the stranger.

"Your boat?" gasped Jim.

"Whose boat did you think it was?" asked the stranger.

"I thought I had bought this boat," said Jim, sagging.

I started to back off the bowsprit.

The stranger slowly went purple.

"I thought you were the painters I'd ordered to come," said he thickly. "Get the heck off of my boat."

We got off.

"The man I got it from," explained Jim, weakly," said it was the second from the end in the row first north of the boathouse."

"What was his name?"

"Henderson."

"You'll find his boat second from the far end of this row," stated the stranger gruffly.

"Why," said Jim, "that's a motor cruiser."

"Your boat is between the cruiser and the end boat," said the stranger.

Jim led me down the row. And there, on the ground, hidden down between a large sloop and the pot-bellied motor cruiser, was a measly little clinker-built sort of a cat boat, faded and scuffed, a kind of a slightly over-size dinghy, flat on the ground like a dying duck.

"Oh," moaned Jim.

"A sloop?" I asked, hushed.

"Oh, oh," moaned Jim. And he walked rapidly back up the row to the gentleman who was still surveying his ship.

"How about the paint I put on your boat?" Jim asked.

"How about scraping that paint off my boat?" barked the sea dog.

And in silence Jim, carrying the pail of paint and I following with the white pail, led to our waiting car.

"How about your boat, Jim?" I asked.

"My boat?" said Jim. "I haven't any boat."

"Haven't you bought it?"

"The guy is coming in for his cheque in the morning," said Jim. "Huh. A sloop. I'll sloop him."

"Sloop," I echoed contemptuously.

And flirting the sand with our tires, we wheeled the car and drove haughtily off the beach back on to the Lake Shore Rd. without even a glance at the dimpling blue lake.

From the frying pan, Pierre ladled us our trout . . . And, with glittering eyes, watched us as we tasted our first bite.

Food For Thought

May 28, 1938

"Heigh-ho, heigh-ho," sang Jimmie Frise, "it's off to eat we go!"

And he came swinging in the early evening along the water side, a stick with five nice trout on it dangling from his hand.

"Quitting already?" I called from midstream.

"This is all I can eat," he replied, holding up the trout. They were about the size to fit neatly across a frying pan.

"Why, the evening rise is just about to begin," I protested, waving my rod and flicking a neat cast along the far bank.

"How many have you got?" called Jim.

"I too have five," I informed him proudly.

"Well, then, let's go out to the car and eat," suggested Jim. "Before it gets dark. And we can be back at the cabin before midnight."

"And miss the best of the evening rise?" I demanded.

"Look," said Jim, "it's a warm evening. These trout won't keep and we've got all day tomorrow to catch trout to take home. Let's go out to the car and have a feed on these."

I waded ashore in order to consider the question without prejudice. Standing waist deep in a beautiful trout stream is no condition in which to be passionate.

"Jim," I said, propping the fly rod and sinking down on the soft bank, "a man can eat any time. But only once in a while, and for only a little period of his life, can a man go fishing."

"We've had a swell day," countered Jim, also sagging down on the pleasant bank, and I'd like to top it off with a nice mess of fried trout."

"Until he is 30," I stated, " a man is too young to fish for trout. After 50, a man is too old."

"Too old?" scoffed Jim.

"Yes," I explained. "Until a man is 30, he has no real appreciation of the finer things of life. He is just a bundle of prime beef and energy. He goes, like a young bull, rampaging at life, with nary a moment's pause to taste, to savor; to reflect upon the charm and beauty of life. About 30, a man starts to be conscious of faint thrills and quivers within him, which are the first premonitions of the increasing beauty and the increasing sadness of life. All during his '30s and '40s a man lives in a kind of symphony of feeling, a sort of grand orchestral suite of sensation, with largos and adagios and scherzos . . ."

"Spik Eenglish?" inquired Jim sweetly.

"What I mean," I corrected, "in his '30s and '40s a man balances his energies with his powers of appreciation and gets a feeling of the fulness of life. Around 50, he begins

to slow up and get working on a simple formula of life.
He starts, at 50, to cut his life down to some simple rou-
tine that he knows, from experience, will give him the
most pleasure for the least effort—because he is beginning to fade."

An Instant of Beauty

"Look at that river," interrupted Jim.

And the little river was indeed something more than a
picture. It was a mood. An instant of beauty. A sort of
living combination of earth, rock, water and sky, of time
and air and hour, of some subtle combination of all the
forces of nature to make an instant of beauty, as though
a bell had rung, a magic and mellow bell and we sat, en-
tranced, looking, hearing, feeling its swift and passing
vibration.

"There you are, Jim," I said quietly, when the mood
that touched us both had passed. "When you were 30 you
wouldn't have noticed that instant of beauty. You would
merely have seen a river, and charged into it rod ram-
pant to bang at the fish."

"O.K. then," said Jim, "let us go now out to the car and
have supper."

"I would like merely to add," I said, defeated, though
the plops of trout in the smooth flowing little river were
becoming more frequent as the evening rise began. "I
would merely like to say that at 60 men reduce their appreciation of life the way great singers reduce their rep-
ertoire. Women who have sung the greatest operas, the
greatest roles, Isolde, Mimi, who have stood in massive
halls before uncounted thousands of ravished listeners,
presently feel their powers declining, and at the last
they appear on farewell tours and sing Annie Laurie. It
is the same with fishing. In a few years, Jimmie, you and
I will not come away out here to fish. We will join fishing
clubs and fish in puddles."

"Let's eat," said Jim drily. He is a trifle nearer 50 than
I am.

We stood for a little while, gratefully and reverently
looking at the stream, its queer quiet purpose, its air of
infinity, as though it had always run and always would

run forever. And the trees and shrubs seemed to stand guard over it and lean down to embrace it, and the sky appeared to be coloring itself only to be mirrored in the dancing secret water.

"Come on," said Jim; and we started out.

"As a matter of fact, Jim," I said, batting mosquitoes, "this is the poorest part of a fishing trip, this eating, this coming to the end of a perfect day with canned beans in a frying pan."

"Fried trout, you mean," amended Jim, swinging up his catch to show me. They had dried somewhat, losing their bluish and jewelled lustre. They had lost their shape, too; lost that dynamic plumpness that so entrances the trout fisherman's eye. "Ah, Jim," I sighed, "even fried trout. We have dramatized fried trout, we anglers. It is in memory and in prospect that fried trout taste good. But as a matter of fact, the way we cook them, they either stick to the pan or are as dry as corrugated paper or else half raw."

"Aw," said Jim, walking ahead on the trail. "Spoil everything, go ahead."

"I'm sorry, Jim, but face the facts," I pursued, hurrying to keep up with him. "These trout we've got, inside of an hour will be nothing but a brown, burned, crisp, tasteless . . ."

"Shut up," said Jim fiercely over his shoulder, and he strode furiously ahead along the trail so that I didn't bother trying to catch up. Trails are not for arguing, anyway, for at this hour of the day, the hermit thrushes are starting their arpeggios, and maybe if a man is lucky, a rose-breasted grosbeak will sing his baritone robinsong from a tree top in the evening sunlight. When we came out of the trail into the old abandoned field across which we could see our car by the road, Jim was standing waiting for me.

"What's up?" he asked, pointing.

From beside our car, the smoke of a campfire was curling faint and blue. And beside our car moved the figure of a man, busy with the fire.

"That's funny," I said. "No other car there."

We walked together across the field and as we came

nearer, we saw that the man beside our car was a most unprepossessing individual.

"A regular hobo," muttered Jim.

The gent did not see us approaching, but was busily shifting stones, making some sort of a fireplace, and he had gathered quite a pile of dry wood.

"What's all this?" said Jim, as we came within earshot.

"Ah," cried the hobo, dramatically, "Here you are."

"Yes, here we are," I admitted sourly.

"You got some trout, I hope?" said the hobo, whose voice and manner seemed elaborately polite for such a dilapidated exterior.

"Yes, we got some trout," agreed Jim, as if to inquire what business it was of his.

"I regret," said the hobo ceremoniously, "that I could not get into your car to extract the luncheon and the cooking utensils."

He smiled so engagingly from his plump and stubbled face that, to tell the truth, we didn't know what to say.

"Gentlemen," he said, "this is nothing new to me but I fear it is new to you. I . . . am a chef."

"Hmm," said I, looking at his hands, which were, I am happy to report, clean and trim.

"Yes, sir, a chef," said the hobo, pulling at his jacket a little elegantly. "And it is my habit, in the summer, to travel roads where sportsmen are likely to be found. And whenever I come upon a car, such as yours, and realizing how hungry the sportsmen are likely to be when they come out, and so weary . . ."

He paused, lifting his eyebrows dramatically but with a slightly bizarre effect of elegance.

"Well, gentlemen, at any rate, with your kind permission, may I prepare your supper? And in return may I partake of a small portion of what is left?"

Jim nudged me. I nudged back.

"So you're a chef?" said Jim.

"I have cooked for royalty," said the hobo. "I have held the highest rank in some of the greatest hotels in the world, both Europe and America. You may call me Pierre, if you wish."

"Well, er, ah," said Jimmie, "I'm afraid we haven't much for you to go on here in the car . . ."

"Tttt, ttt, tttt," cried Pierre, "you have some trout. What more is needed?"

"We've got a large can of beans," said Jim, starting to unlock the car door, "and some bread and a small pickle bottle full of butter, if it hasn't melted . . ."

"Ttttt, tttt," cried Pierre, pinching his thumb and finger together in the ancient and approved gesture of chefs, "please, gentlemen, just give me the freedom of the car and leave all to me. I am accustomed to what is to be found in sportsmen's cars."

Jim started to hand out the carton and the packages and parcels, but Pierre politely elbowed Jim aside.

"Gentlemen," he said, "may I suggest that there is a small brook crossing the road down about 50 yards. If you stroll down there, for a wash and a splash, and take your time . . ."

So we laid our rods aside and started off, I observing with some rising of the heart, that the fireplace Pierre had constructed with a few rocks, was a very workman-like job, an improvement, as a matter of fact, on the classic campfire invented and detailed by the famous Ness-muk in his book *Woodcraft*. The stones were skilfully spaced, a large stone for a backlog had been rolled into place and between the sides a hot small fire of solid glowing embers hummed redly.

Golden and Blue

"Jim," I said low, as we walked down the road, "I kind of like that guy."

"Did you ever hear of such a trick to get a free meal?" asked Jim.

"There's nothing for him to go on," I pointed out. "That can of beans, a loaf of bread, some sour pickles, tea, and sugar."

"And a lemon," added Jim, "for the tea."

"Oh, well," I pointed out, "he can't cook them any worse than we would."

With which thought, we reached the little brook passing under a small log bridge, and there in the gin-clear water we washed and splashed our faces, and Jim found a piece of comb in his pocket, which we shared.

"Give him time," said Jim, as we started back up the road. So instead of turning in by the car, we paced side by side on up the road, while Pierre signalled us eagerly and appreciatively.

"That's it, gentlemen," he called. "Walk up and down that delightful road and I will call you when all is prepared."

"I'll be jiggered," breathed Jim. "If this isn't the strangest thing."

We strolled slowly up the evening road, amid the tall trees, like two gentlemen strolling on the terrace outside some palace of the Riviera, though our ragged fishing clothes were hardly formal, and no stringed instruments beguiled us but only the reeds and woodwinds of the bush, the birds, the spring peepers and the tree toads. Three times we passed the car, each time, bent above the fire in a fury, Pierre glanced anxiously up and shook a warning hand at us not to approach.

Then, just as we found a bittern down by that log bridge over the brook, and were listening with perennial astonishment to the "bittern with his bump," that sound like a squeaky pump, we heard a far hail from Pierre, and all aglow we strode back up the road.

"Forty minutes," said Jim. "That's what he's taken."

But oh, my friends and oh, my foes, what else had he taken but our very hearts? From a piece of newspaper, Pierre had constructed himself a chef's hat, or a passable replica thereof. All around him, as he stood proudly beaming, were spread dishes, our frying pan, a covered pot which Pierre had produced from his own dilapidated packsack; a birchbark platter of crisp watercress from the brook.

"Be seated, gentlemen," said Pierre bowing to the running board of the car. "Or have you, perhaps a toast you wish to name before you sit."

"Here," said Jim, "is to . . . to everything!"

We sat. Pierre handed us each one of our own tin plates. From the frying pan, in which lay our trout, not crisp, not brown, but golden and blue, their native glory showing, all simmering in a sharp brown sauce . . . rose with an aroma that fairly made us gasp.

From the pot, he ladled out, round white objects . . .

"Potatoes?" I remarked.

"No, sir," cried Pierre, "the root of the common arrow-head that grows in shallow water along all our ponds and creeks. I make it my habit to gather such delicacies as the wild wood affords, in my travels."

With glittering eyes, the eyes of the artist Pierre watched us as we lifted the first bite.

Even his stubble seemed to vanish when we lifted our amazed eyes after that bite.

"Eh?" he asked, breathless. "That little tang is crinkle-root, that I picked right here by the road, and a faint dash of Indian turnip, that you call jack-in-the-pulpit. A little watercress was cooked in that sauce . . . eh? . . . and a dash of your lemon. It gives it a . . ."

"My Greatest Joy"

But even Pierre grew silent as he watched us. This was no occasion for haste. Each lift of the fork, each opening of the mouth, each closing of the jaws had to be done slowly, rhythmically, with rolling eyeballs and deep inhales.

"The last time," I finally breathed, "was at the coronation, Pierre, at Scott's, in Piccadilly, and it was Sole a la Scott."

"This," said Pierre, "is trout a la Pierre."

"My dear man," said Jim, huskily, "I know hotel managers, I know proprietors of summer hotels where I could get you a good job."

"Tttt, tttt," cried Pierre, "no, no, gentlemen, do not make that mistake. I was a chef for 30 years. I have been cribbed, cabined and confined most of my life; a happy life, too. But some years ago, deep in the copper-lined bowels of a great hotel, as I stood amidst my masterpieces, I suddenly thought, as Saul must have thought on the road to Damascus . . . 'What am I doing here?' So I just packed a small bag and walked away."

"We could get you . . ." I began.

"Nobody," said Pierre, "can get me anything. That is my greatest joy in the world. Nobody can get me anything. And I can get something for others."

We resumed our eating. Pierre heaped bunches of crisp cress on our plates and laid fresh trout on top, and poured that indescribable sauce from the pan over them.

"Where will you be," asked Jim, "a week from today, Pierre?"

"Please God," said Pierre, "five-hundred miles from here."

"We'll be back here," I pleaded, "tomorrow."

"Ah," smiled Pierre, "tomorrow, a hundred miles from here. No, gentlemen, that is the essence of freedom. To make no plans nor enter into any agreements. It is my delight to walk the roads and find the cars of sportsmen and have a fire ready and their food laid out when they return from the woods. No men are hungrier. No men are more appreciative. What an artist craves is appreciation. You cannot know, gentlemen, what happiness you have given me by eating this food."

He ladled out another lily root for each of us, and bathed it in the sauce, which he had mysteriously augmented with more butter and a squirt of lemon and a tiny dash of some mashed herb.

Instead of tea, he had made us coffee, out of his own packsack. Coffee that was pure liquid aroma.

"Now, while I eat," he said, "I suggest you go for another walk on the road."

It was a command not a request, so we went, and hands behind, and minds bewildered with thoughts of freedom, and bodies all aglow from the power of beautiful food, we paced up and down the twilight road, until the whip-poor-wills began and we heard Pierre cleaning up the pans.

"Let us drive you," we pleaded, "part of the way you're going."

"You can't go," said Pierre, gently, "the way I'm going."

And we all shook hands and he went one way and we went the other.

145

Kum-On-In

July 16, 1938

"No more fooling," said Jimmie Frise; "you've got to come down with me this weekend to visit Uncle Jake and Aunt Minnie on the farm."

"What crop are they gathering this week?" I inquired bitterly.

"I picked this week specially," said Jim, "because there are no crops. The hay is in. The farm is at rest for a little while now. You will see the farm at its best. The cattle fat and clean. The fields bright and heavy."

"Three times," I stated firmly, "I have visited the farm with you. Once there was threshing. Once there was haying. And the third time Uncle Jake had the lumbago."

"That was in my mind," said Jim apologetically. "My idea in going down this week is that there is nothing whatever doing on the farm. I haven't heard from Uncle Jake since Christmas. That means he is in good health. The only time he writes is when he is in pain. It relieves him to write a letter when he has something wrong with him."

"I've never visited a farm in summer," I confessed. "In

"Welcome, strangers," cried Uncle Jake. "You're just in time. Only one cabin left. And it's a dandy one at that."

147

summer we're always summer resorting. We visit farms in autumn, when they are forlorn."

"Exactly," said Jim. "More than three-quarters of the people of the world live on farms. The whole basis of human civilization is the farm, not the shop or the factory or the town. I think we owe it to ourselves, as seekers after the truth, however silly it turns out to be in the end, to know something about farms other than what we can see jazzing along highways at fifty miles an hour."

"You're quite right," I agreed.

"Sometimes," said Jim a little wistfully, "I sort of half regret having left the farm to become a cartoonist. There is a false glamor to town and city life. It doesn't pay, in the end. You run away from the farm to escape manual labor, driving horses, handling forks, steering plows. You imagine it is a far better thing to be a mechanic in a factory, standing beside a machine. Or sitting on a stool in an office. You see a city's street cars, its pavements, its lights and conveniences, its gaiety, its endless activity. And what do you give away in exchange?"

"I don't like getting up at 5 a.m.," I pointed out.

"Pah," said Jim bitterly. "It isn't that. It is the peace and freedom you lose. It is the quiet and the gentleness. The patience and the kindly waiting. You plow, you plant and you tend and watch. All things come home. The wheat ripens in due season. The calves are born to the very day. Morning comes and night drops down. It is a life of order and beauty, and it is ordered not by the will of man but by the serene and eternal laws of nature. We are a long step nearer to Heaven on the farm; and in cities it's a long, long step the other way."

Chicken and Rhubarb Pie

"When a city man comes into my office to see me," I confided, "he sits down on the edge of the chair and is half risen to go all in the same movement. But when a friend from the farm comes in, he enters slowly, waiting to see the impression of pleasure and delight on my face, reflecting his own. He looks about to see where to hang his hat. He selects a chair and draws it forward to a pleasant and comfortable position. He relaxes. He is there for an hour. And I, who love him, must sit, all strangely and uneasily relaxed, wondering how I can tell him I must hurry, that work is pressing, that I am a squirrel in a cage and must run, run, run round and round. I dare not relax. In cities it is fatal, it is terrible, it is painful, physically painful, to relax."

"How," demanded Jim, "can we ever solve the troubles of the world while the human race is so divided into two races? Two species as distinct as hawks and chickens? Three-quarters of the human race look upon life from the sweet reality of the farm. The other quarter, the deadly, scheming, clever, achieving quarter, look upon life from the dread artificiality of the city?"

"The way it is going now," I suggested, "we are slowly starving a pretty big percentage of people out of the cities. Unemployed. If we keep up the present tendencies, the number of people in cities is going to grow less and less until presently the control, the direction of human affairs, will pass out of the hands of lawyers and promoters and get back into the hands of the majority, the people on the farms."

"Uncle Jake," said Jim, "will be glad to see us. Aunt Minnie will give us a rousing welcome and fly to the kitchen to get some of those famous rhubarb pies of hers into the oven and a chicken on."

"Fried chicken?" I offered.

"Roast chicken," cried Jim, "boiled chicken, fried chicken, young chicken fried American style, chicken fricassee, chicken hash. The times I've been at Uncle Jake's and Aunt Minnie's I eat chicken till I bust, yet I never tire of it. Nobody knows how many ways there are of doing chicken until he has visited a farm in July."

"Cold roast chicken," I gloated.

"Chicken jellied," said Jim, "with thick green lettuce, not the pale kind, but the rich dark green kind with a tang."

"Will we leave Friday night or Saturday morning?" I asked.

And in due time we were headed out the highways for

Uncle Jake's, amidst the city-fleeing throng of week-enders.

"Just look at them," cried Jimmie, as the cars filed away ahead of us and honked their horns wildly to pass us from the long stream behind, "rushing away from the city for just a few hours' taste of what they might have forever on the farm."

"Don't they look silly," I agreed.

"I picked up an Englishman," related Jimmie, "on the Lake Shore road the other morning. Do you know how he spends his weekends? There are some of these dinky tourist camps right on the outskirts of Toronto. They are meant to accommodate tourists coming to or passing through Toronto, in lieu of hotels. This Englishman, on Saturday afternoons, goes out to one of these suburban tourist camps, hires a cabin for Saturday and Sunday nights, $1 a night, and gets into his bathing suit."

"I can see him," I admitted, "tall and knobby."

The Gipsy in Human Nature

"And there he is, ten minutes outside of the city," continued Jim, "in the green country, with a beach nearby, with people in holiday mood all around him. He bathes in the sun and the lake. He has the camp owner bring him tea and toast Sunday morning, while he lies in bed in the little cubby. He has a swell time for about $2.50, counting car tickets. And he wants to know why people have to rush off a hundred miles for a week-end?"

"Not a tourist camp, Jim," I begged. "Don't suggest that we forego a lovely weekend visit to the Muskoka Lakes in favor of a visit to a tourist camp."

"They say they're not half bad," submitted Jim.

"My dear man," I protested, "ridiculous as all these cars look, streaming in all directions madly from the city at this hour, they look far less ridiculous than people going 10 miles from a comfortable bed to cramp themselves into a tourist cubby."

"Think it over," advised Jim. "This tourist cabin business is on the increase. This whole trailer cabin idea is growing by leaps and bounds. We are just seeing the beginning of it now. In winter, all over the southern part of

150

the states, there are whole cities of trailers and tourist cabins. Mark my words, in the summer, we are going to see whole cities of them up here."

"It isn't human nature," I informed him, "to live in a shack. Human nature craves property, space, room."

"Wrong," cried Jimmie. "Like so many other ideas about human nature, that one is utterly wrong. Human nature is tired of property, tired of possessions that anchor them down. Men are discovering that to be anchored to a house is like being anchored to a mountain."

"Jim, that's heresy," I stated. "What would real estate men and trust companies say to that?"

"You can't change human nature," insisted Jim. "You can twist it out of shape for a century or two, maybe, but it works itself back to normal in time. And I tell you, the natural man likes a shanty, a shack, a cubby, a cave, one room, just enough to keep him warm and dry and space to store his hunting tools. That is the natural man, not this queer jackdaw, this collector of trinkets and baubles that is supposed to be the normal man today."

"You're subversive, Jim," I warned him.

"We must try one of those tourist camps some time," said Jim.

"Not me," I assured him. "Not me. With people jammed in all around you, people you don't know, never saw before and never will see again, yet your most intimate neighbors for a night. And kids yelling and snores from both sides shaking the flimsy walls. No, sirree! And early birds on their way at daybreak and people coming in late, stumbling and banging against your cabin at three a.m. No, sirree!"

"I'd like to have a try at it," repeated Jimmie, and we both craned our necks to look at a handsome array of brand new tourist cabins at a road corner as we sailed along. There were merry groups of people amidst the aisles of the cabins, and cars half unloaded and children romping and women doing washing and hanging clothes on tiny lines.

"It's the gipsy in human nature coming out," said Jim.

151

"Ah," I cried, pointing to a farm all lush and green, the white farm house bowered with bending trees, aloof, serene. "But look at that. There's the real thing."

"Plus chicken," admitted Jim. "Plus chicken hash on toast."

"Cold roast chicken," I corrected, "broken apart by hand. Not sliced. Just broken into gobbets."

"Mmmmmm," we harmonized. I pushed down a little on the gas and joined with the endless streams of those escaping from Nineveh and Tyre, nor ever looking back.

And in a couple of hours of this stewing and grinding, we left the beaten path and took the second-class road that led to Uncle Jake's. It was still a beaten path, however, for few and far between are the roads nowadays that are not beaten.

"Hurray," we yelled when we topped the last hill and saw ahead the cluster of elms and maples that are the symbol of the peace and plenty amidst which Uncle Jake resides.

"There's somebody there," exclaimed Jim. "See the cars in the lane."

"Maybe he's holding a sale of stock," I offered.

"There's nobody to be married," muttered Jim. "I hope it isn't a funeral."

Startling Changes

And with every yard we grew nearer to Uncle Jake's lane, the more anxious we felt. Because there was certainly something going on at Uncle Jake's. We could see cars parked not only in the lane but around the house.

"Good heavens," shouted Jim, so suddenly that I took my foot off the gas and coasted. "Tourist camp."

And now we could see the back of the house behind which was a bright array. A vivid and bright avenue of little tourist shacks, amidst which a quiet population moved in the supper time light.

"Are you sure it's Uncle Jake's place?" I enquired.

"Did I never spend my happy boyhood here?" said Jim brokenly.

As we turned in the lane, we could see Uncle Jake politely and ceremoniously waving us onward, a true greeter.

"Oh, ho, ho," cried Jim, tragically.

I drove slowly in. Children romped and leaped, a man with a banjo played whanging tunes, folks were at supper and Aunt Minnie greeted us in a great swither of excitement and joy.

"Chicken dinner, 50 cents," said a sign on the gate as we rolled funereally through.

"Welcome, strangers," cried Uncle Jake, stepping on the running board. "You're just in the nick of time. Only one cabin left. And a dandy at that. Turn left."

We turned left and drove along the turf.

"Here you are," said Uncle Jake, swinging athletically off and waving a hand at just another of the gaudy little shanties.

"Uncle Jake," said Jim, "my friend here is troubled with hayfever and asthma. He isn't allowed to sleep in cabins. How about that room I used to be in, when I was a kid? The one with the sloping ceiling and the big red flowers on the wallpaper?"

"Aw, Jimmie," said Uncle Jake, "that's let. We've got some semi-permanent guests up in that room."

"There's nothing but these?" asked Jim earnestly, as a nephew to an uncle.

"Why, what's the matter with these?" cried Uncle Jake. "A dollar a night? Paid in advance? A dry, well-built, cosy little kumfy kabin like this?"

"How about it?" asked Jim turning to me.

"Where else would we go?" I retorted grimly.

We got out and Uncle Jake helped us with our stuff.

"I hate to charge you boys," said he, confidentially when we got inside. It was hot and smelt of new wood. "I hate to charge my own kinfolks, but you see how it is. I'm in business. I got to get my income from the investment. Now, if you had come during the week, I might have let you off. But the weekend is my busy time . . ."

"It's all right," said Jim, "what's a dollar between relatives?"

"Well, it's quite exciting," said Uncle Jake, patting the

153

walls and door admiringly. "Farming is no good any more. This is the line of business everybody ought to be in on the farm. I figure I won't be doing any plowing or seeding next spring at all, at the rate it's coming in now."

"We're Living At Last"

"Well, one thing," said Jim, sitting down on the narrow stretcher on his side of the cabin, "we'll have a chicken dinner. And has Aunt Minnie got any rhubarb pies?"

"Oh, shoot," said Uncle Jake, snapping his fingers, "we're just out of chickens. This crowd ate up the whole supply we had ready and I haven't another on the place that ain't laying."

"No chicken?" I said. "No cold bits left over?"

"Not a scrap of chicken," said Uncle Jake. "I only got a few layers left. I got to buy my chickens in town now, the whole neighborhood is fresh out of chickens due to this kind of business."

"How about rhubarb pie?" asked Jim. "One of Aunt Min's famous brown-top rhubarb pies?"

"Jimmie," said Uncle Jake, part way out the door and all ready to fly in answer to a car horn tooting in the distance, "Minnie is that busy looking after the place we've had to get a girl in specially to do the cooking. She'll put you up a nice feed, though. when you're set, come to the kitchen and see her. Fifty cents only, for supper."

He vanished, his boots crunching hurriedly.

Jim leaned his elbows on his knees and buried his face in his hands. He sat a long time so, while I arranged my belongings around the camp stretcher on my side of the cubby.

After awhile, he sat up and we went to the kitchen where a large, strange girl laid us out a nice meal of potted meat and mashed potatoes, pickles and buns. But it seemed as if neither thought nor imagination had been given to the meal. The girl just took the stuff off the pantry shelves as her hand found them. They were not viands aimed at us, as individuals. They were food for anybody.

Aunt Minnie swept furiously through the kitchen several times, all flushed and full of vim. She embraced Jim heartily.

"Oh, Jim," she said, "we're having the grandest time!"

"The old place is all changed," said Jim.

"And wasn't it time?" cried Aunt Minnie. "Why, we're living at last."

After supper, Uncle Jake told us to walk around and look the old place over. In the barn were three cows and a horse. A couple of pigs had the look of being fed on chocolate bars and sandwiches. Jim showed me where there used to be 15 cows that he had helped milk. He walked me over fields where he had hunted wary groundhogs as a boy; and now the groundhogs whistled at us scornfully.

We came back at dusk and found two trailer cabins had joined the community, just for company. We sat on the step of our cubby, and watched the strange phenomenon of neighbors for a night, this weird society based on hours instead of years. There was music and singing and children yelling to bed and banging and engines and a game of horseshoes. There was advancing night and a gathering quiet. There were snores and mutters and the going out of lights.

"When it is all quiet," whispered Jim, under the stars that were over the brooding elms, "we'll get the heck out of here."

Which we did.

The Complete Anglers

August 6, 1938

"His plug hit my hat, lifted it from my head and flung it 12 feet away."

"Will you help me," inquired Jimmie Frise, "catch frogs?"

"I will not." I informed him emphatically.

"You're a lot closer to the ground than I am," complained Jim. "I don't see why you wouldn't help a friend catch a frog or two."

"I object to it," I stated, "on all grounds. I can't think of even one reason why I should help you catch those poor little devils that after all look more like human beings than even monkeys do."

"We could go fishing sooner," proposed Jim. "That's one good reason for helping me catch them. It takes me an hour to catch 10 frogs."

"Why don't you give up bait fishing," I asked, "and take up casting artificial lures, like plugs or spoons? It's so far more effective and 10 times the fun."

"I do cast," protested Jimmie indignantly.

"Yah," I said. "Side-swiping. You don't call that casting."

"I get the line out," declared Jim.

"You side-swipe," I informed him. "You side-swipe, you grab the rod and take a swing any old way and hope for the best. You endanger the lives of everybody around you in boat or on wharf. And no man living, much less you, can tell where the bait is going."

"I've caught plenty of fish casting," stated Jim.

"If you," I said, "can catch plenty of fish side-swiping and flummoxing the plug around, how many more fish could you catch if you would only make an honest effort to learn how to cast properly, over your head?"

"I like fishing with a frog," pleaded Jimmie. "It's the old-fashioned way. Bass love frogs. I hate to fool a bass with a hunk of painted wood."

"You hypocrite," I hissed.

"Well, anyway," said Jim, "I give him an even break. I toss him a frog. If he gets the frog off the hook he at least has got something for his trouble. But what do you cast him? Just a hunk of painted wood or a little blade of brass or copper. And if he does succeed in taking that off you

157

what good is it to him?"

"You quibbler," I grated.

"Fishing," said Jim, "is like religion. If you don't do it the way I do, you're wrong. Why not let me fish my way and you fish your way and we'll all have fun?"

"Fine," I agreed. "But don't expect me to go creeping and pouncing through the long grass, chasing poor little green frogs for you."

"I only suggested that you help me, to save time," said Jim. "And anyway, you're good at catching frogs. Back in the old days before you went high brow and started bait casting, you used to be able to catch more frogs than all the rest of us put together."

"I have too many frogs on my conscience now," I muttered. "I don't want to add to the burden on my soul. Thousands of frogs. Baby frogs. I feel like King Herod."

The Right Way Is So Easy

"Aw, a frog has no feelings," said Jim. "Hardly any. Nature made frogs to feed herons, fish, snakes and people like that. If they were made for food, it stands to reason nature didn't equip them with much feelings. The more rarely a creature is eaten, the higher are its sensibilities. That's true isn't it?"

"It is true," I admitted. "But I am not thinking so much of feelings as of life itself. Life is just as dear to that little frog as it is to us. We may have a little deeper feeling for life, but a frog is just as full of that feeling as we are in proportion. I hate to take a frog's life."

"How about taking a fish's life?" cried Jim.

"That's different," I guarded. "To take a frog's life in order to take a fish's life, that seems to me doubly damned."

"You have taken thousands of lives from fish," said Jim. "Do you feel no compunction about that? Doesn't it ever twinge your conscience?"

"Not in the least," I defended. "In taking a fish's life. I am relieving it from a very miserable, wet and slimy existence. Think of the life a fish must lead, forever down in that cold, dark chasm of the water. Beset by enemies of every kind, including his own kind. A fish lives in terror every hour of its life, from the minute it is hatched from the egg, a tiny helpless wriggler, until it ends at least the victim of my lure, deceitful, clever and skilled."

"I imagine fish get used to living in the water," said Jim. "Anybody can get used to his environment in time."

"No, sir," I said. A frog, especially a little bright green frog with gold markings on him lives a happy life in the shining grass alongside a lively sandy beach. Amid sunlight and pretty flies iridescent in the sun, he swells, and whenever he feels like it, he hops down and goes for a swim in the cool, lilied water. But a fish lives in shadow and gloom, in weeds and slime and cold. Beset with terrors, he slinks his way to maturity, and when he reaches maturity, what has he got? Does he escape from his lowly element? Like aquatic insects, does he emerge from the water, a slimy thing, and shed his skin, to become a light and airy dancer in the evening sunlight for a day? No. He grows old and scaly and scabby and mouldy and dies. Unless . . . "

"Ah, unless," said Jim.

"Unless I," I said, "or some other humane soul comes along and rescues him from his unhappy lot."

"With a painted plug," said Jim.

"Or a good copper casting spoon," I suggested, since I had decided to use a spoon fishing today.

"O.K.," said Jim. "I'll cast."

"Not side-swiping?" I protested.

"You cast your way, I'll cast my way," said Jim.

"My dear boy," I said. "It is so easy to learn to cast a plug overhead. The correct way. It is like throwing an apple off a pointed stick."

"I never could get on to it," said Jim.

"Look," I said. "Rest your thumb firmly on the spooled line, see? That holds the plug dangling six inches from the tip of the rod. Point the rod in the direction you wish to cast. Then, with a short, smart upward movement, not forceful but swinging, cut an arc over your right shoulder, straight back to a little past the vertical."

"I see it, so far," agreed Jim. "Now what?"

"Not now what," I protested vehemently. "It isn't two motions. It is one continuous motion, back and forward."

"That's where I go wrong," agreed Jim.

One Continuous Motion

"It is where nearly everybody goes wrong who can't cast," I informed him. "They make two distinct motions of the cast. They lay the rod back over their shoulder. They stop. Then they make a chuck forward. That isn't it at all. It is one continuous motion, that throwing of the rod back and flinging it forward."

"Let me see?" said Jim taking my rod, with the spoon already on it for casting.

"You sort of bounce the plug forward," I explained. "You use the spring of the rod. It is all very gentle and simple. No force. No chucking. You just swing the rod in an arc, over your shoulder, and instantly forward again, gently relaxing, but NOT releasing, the pressure of your thumb on the spooled line."

"Ah, you don't let go of the line?" cried Jim.

"Never," I assured him. "That is what causes backlashes, or snarls. You just relax the pressure of your thumb enough to let the plug fly high and smooth through the air. You watch it sail out, feeling, gently, with your thumb the dwindling spool of line under it."

"I think I've got it," said Jim.

And standing forth and taking a deep breath, he swung the rod a few times back and forward and then, with a sudden effort, slashed forward with the rod. The spoon jerked wildly through the air for eight feet and then spanked ignominiously to earth. The reel was just a bird's nest, just a great tumbled tangle of line.

"I must have let go my thumb," muttered Jim.

"You didn't," I informed him. "You put enough energy into that forward cast to throw a cat over a barn. I tell you, make one continuous motion of the back and forward throw of the rod, and the plug bounces, without effort, really, straight and smooth through the air."

"I'll try again," said Jim, picking at the backlash. He got it cleared up and re-wound evenly on the spool. He tried a few more practice swings and then, the same as before, hurled all his muscles, from the balls of his feet to the back of his neck, into a violent forward shoot.

The spoon streaked forward in a blur of speed, curved back like a yo-yo ball, then dangled to a stop around the rod.

"Tch, tch," I said, "You've done the same thing all over again!"

"Here," rasped Jim. "Take your rod, I'll do it my way. I can get it out as slick as syrup from a bottle my way. Your way is just fancy. Just a fishing refinement."

"It is not a refinement," I stated. "It is the only way to cast not only for the safety of others, but for accuracy. You don't know where your lure is going if you chuck it sideways."

"Fish are likely to be any place," argued Jim. "Just as likely in the place my plug lands as in the place I try to land it."

"We will go in separate boats," I ordained.

"Let's go together," pleaded Jim, "so that I can watch you and perhaps profit by observation."

"In that case," I agreed. So we went together in the same punt, and proceeded with the pleasurable sport of bait casting. It is a comparatively new sport. It has the fascination of golf, in that there is the test of where you want them. But happily, unlike golf, you do not have to walk hopelessly after your shots, you merely reel them back into you, sitting. The art of bait casting from a multiplying reel and short rod was developed in Kentucky by the bass fishermen of the '90s. At first, they cast their metal spoons, live minnows, frogs and other baits, weighting them to about three-quarters of an ounce, to make a nice weight to fling. About 1900, the wooden minnow or "plug" began to appear and today, there are hundreds of patterns, brilliantly painted creations, with three sets of treble gang hooks. They wobble in the water as they are being reeled in, and whether a fish takes them for food or merely out of curiosity, like the

161

angler who bought them in the store, nobody knows, because I get most of my fish on the plugs that look the least like anything. The less it looks like something, the better it is.

I gave Jim the whole of the boat except the stern. I took the stern seat and huddled down in it, so that Jim, with his side-swiping, could have the whole world to himself.

"Now watch," he said, rising to stand unsteadily in the punt.

And with a vicious looping side cut, he lashed his rod horizontally through the air, the plug flying savagely over the water to land, much to Jim's astonishment, 30 feet to the left of where he intended it to go.

"Good," he said. "That's a better spot than the one I intended."

And slowly he reeled the plug home, watching intently for the strike of the fish.

But no fish struck, as indeed, is usually the case, and rightly so. If fish came easy, who would fish except fish dealers? It is the casting that is the fun, saved from monotony now and then at long intervals by the sudden and wholly unexpected interruption of a fish. I suppose the average man casts 500 times for one fish landed. Perhaps a thousand.

Without ostentation, I did my overhead casting steadily and slowly and with intense pleasure. I laid my spoon precisely where I wanted it, or nearly so; along rock and ledge, stump and lily pad, as slick and trim as Ivanhoe ever laid his arrows, or nearly so. And with a whooshing sound and a fury of bodily effort, Jim swung and swiped and startled the great open spaces of water with the plunging arrival of his gaudy wooden plug. Once it snarled and the plug leaped back into the boat narrowly missing my leg.

"Let me out," I said, "at the next point. I'll be safer on land."

But just then from a cottage veranda a young lad hailed us.

"There's a nice bass hanging around our boat house," he called. "See if you can catch it."

And Jim, hastily reversing his stance, turned to face the boat house, side-swiped with power and his plug hit my hat and lifted it from my head and flung it 12 feet away in the water.

"Gee, I'm sorry," said Jimmie.

"You'd be a funny one if you weren't," I said thinly.

"I never did that before," said Jim, reeling my hat back into the boat.

"You never will again," I informed him, "not the same person, anyway. Row ashore."

"Listen, cast and get that bass," begged Jim.

"Row ashore," I commanded, in a Basil Rathbone sort of a voice.

So Jim rowed ashore, looking very flushed.

"Now, my friend," I announced, as we stepped ashore, "take off one of your socks."

"What for?" demanded Jim.

"For a frog bag," I advised crisply.

So Jim removed one of his socks and we went frog hunting. It is not a knack. It is rather a comprehension. You see your little frog. You transfix it with a trance-like gaze. You stoop slowly to a squatting posture. All in the same lithe, effortless motion, your right arm is extended. It is a continuous motion. Your right hand reaches out in the air over the little creature, whose tiny intelligence seems to be paralyzed by the slow, rhythmic motions. In the same instant, your hand suddenly halts. The frog seems to tense. Then you dart your open hand straight down, not to where the frog was, but to where he is, in mid-air, about four inches straight ahead of where he was sitting when the manoeuvre began.

We got eight frogs between us. We returned to the boat and Jim rigged his rod with a sinker, to trail frogs over the side and I sat in reasonable security in the midst of the punt, casting.

And Jimmie caught one bass, four pike, one perch and nine rock bass with his frogs, and I got nothing with my spoon.

Which only goes to prove that it is every man to his own method.

In Holiday Mood

August 13, 1938

"What time," demanded Jimmie Frise, "do you want to leave for home?"

"Let's leave good and early," I submitted, "before we get caught in that awful Sunday night jam."

"How about five o'clock?" suggested Jim.

"Too late," I protested. "We'll just get within about 50 miles of the city by the time the jam is at its height. We'll be two hours going that last 50 miles. In one awful stew."

"Listen," said Jim, "why don't you accept the 20th century for what it's worth. Accept it. Adapt yourself to it. Traffic jams on Sunday night are part of the normal age we live in. Get in tune with it. Don't fight it. Nothing you can do will alter the fact that every Sunday night in summer you have to boil your way home."

"Unless I leave in time to get home ahead of the jam,"

Then a tire somewhere amongst us went bang and whined. "Oh, ho," I said, "some poor beggar has got a blowout." "It's us," said Jim, hollowly.

I pointed out.

"Look," said Jim. "We arrive here at the cottage at 6 p.m. Saturday. And you want to clear out at noon Sunday. It doesn't make sense."

"I'd rather," I explained, "curtail my week-end than wreck my nerves fighting my way home through a midnight traffic war. If anybody would keep in line and let us all get home at 35 miles an hour, it wouldn't be too bad. But there are always those cutter-inners. Those anti-social bounders that leap ahead every time they get a chance, only to have to duck back into traffic again and throw the whole line out of gear for miles back. Those are the bounders. Those are the people that fray my nerves."

"Be one of them, for a change," laughed Jim. "It's fun. It's a sort of game. Be a traffic inner and outer on our way home tonight. Give it a try."

"Not me," I assured him. "You don't gain one mile in 50, and you risk your life and you strain your car and you infuriate all the other people in the line. It isn't so much the stopping and starting that gets me down, in that traffic jam as we near the city. It's those traffic hounders that keep whizzing madly by you, on the wrong side of the road, and every time they have to nose back into traffic when they meet an up-comer, everybody else has to tramp on brakes, slack off and make way for them. One of these days, I'm just not going to make way for one of those babies, and we'll see what happens."

"You're old-fashioned," stated Jim. "All these views you hold about traffic only prove that you don't belong to these times. The true son of the nineteen-thirties has no nerves at all with regard to traffic. If you are in tune with your time, you just don't notice things like traffic bounders. You just sit easy and hop along with the jam as best you can. That's the spirit of the times."

"We'll clear out of here," I informed him, "at 2 p.m., right after lunch."

"I decline," said Jim. "I say we leave right after supper. It is only 115 miles. Even allow three hours for that little distance, we'll be home shortly after dark."

"Two p.m.," I reiterated.

Coming Back is Different

"Look," said Jim, "let's compromise. We'll leave right after an early supper. We can have a swim at four and supper at five and be out of here before six. And then, instead of going home the main highway, we'll take that back road that comes out through the west end."

"It's a gravel road," I demurred. "Dusty."

"It's a swell big highway," retorted Jim. "I know dozens of people around here who never go home any other road. A big wide gravel highway."

"In an open car," I pointed out, "we'd have grit in our teeth all the way."

"They tell me," said Jim, "that hardly anybody ever uses the road. It's the best way to get home. Let's do that. Let's take the fullest advantage of our week-end by staying till evening and then take the back road home. Let the bounders have the smooth highway, we'll take the happy road home."

"I don't care for experimenting," I muttered, "but we'll try it this once."

So we had a pleasant snooze after lunch and then a swim at three, and the children couldn't be found at 5.30 for supper, so we ate a few minutes past six. But it was still the fine shank of the evening when we loaded up our gear in the car and, waving fond farewells, wheeled out the Muskoka road and headed for the highway.

"What did I tell you?" I demanded, as we came in sight of the highway. Cars, like hurrying beetles, were zipping in unsteady streams southward: The evening was full of the weary roar of traffic.

"We only have about 20 miles of this," said Jim, "and then we turn off on to the back road. Relax and take it easy."

So I got to the right of the road and let the bounders bound. I held a comfortable 40 and let the fifties and sixties, with horns blasting and tires ripping and slithering on the far shoulder, race headlong past us.

"I bet those birds," said Jim, "won't be home half an hour ahead of us. They're heading straight into the maelstrom. We're going the lazy back way, and we'll jog into

167

town pleasantly aired, while they have completely lost all the good their week-end in Muskoka has done them. Nerve-wrecked, exhausted, jittery."

It is funny the difference in tone and tune between going up to Muskoka and coming home from Muskoka. Going up, all is jolly and lively. When a man races past you, you smile to think how eagerly he goes to see his family. But coming home, there is no sense of the merry. It is just a lot of bad-tempered people selfishly struggling home.

"What a spirit," I mused, "in which to end the Sabbath Day. It isn't Sunday baseball games or Sunday tennis that the churches ought to be worrying about. It is this Sunday night traffic. Here are hundreds of thousands of people, all ugly, at war, angry and in no Christian spirit whatsoever, profaning the Sabbath more by their state of mind than all the baseball games imaginable."

"The churches," said Jim, "are practical. They can't stop people motoring. But they can stop baseball games."

And as we coasted along, a man stuck his head out of a passing car and shouted at me: "Put a nickel in it."

And a little while later, another youth shouted as he passed:

"Which end does the concrete come out?"

"There you are, Jimmie," I said bitterly. "There's a Christian spirit for you."

"Never mind," consoled Jim, "in a few minutes we'll be turning off on to the gravel."

The Easy Road Home

A few miles south, we came to the town where the gravel highway goes one way and the concrete the other. Already the inpouring side-roads had filled the highway so that, even in this modest country town, there was a solid stream of cars necessitating frequent halts, slow grinds forward in low gear and more halts.

"Take the next turn to the right," said Jim. "Then we're away."

But as we approached the fork, we saw that about half the cars were taking the gravel and half sticking to the pavement. Down the gravel road for miles hung a great dust cloud.

"Look," I protested. "It's jammed too."

"Take it, take it," commanded Jimmie before I could come to any decision. So I took it. With a slither and a bump, we were on the gravel and headed the back way home to Toronto. Ahead, cars fled away in yellow clouds, fencing around each other anxiously for front position. Hardly had we gone 50 yards before two, cars with horns roaring slithered past us, sweeping up vast clouds of dust and flinging pebbles against our windshield.

"So," I said, "we take the easy road home."

"We just happened to get into a bunch," explained Jim. "Wait a few minutes until this crowd get ahead."

So I slackened speed and let the dust-flingers move farther out. But, one by one, fresh cars came rushing from behind, as if each driver hoped to get ahead of all the others and so escape the dust.

"This is going to be a dandy drive home," I assured Jim. "We should have left at two p.m., as I advised."

"It's just a coincidence," said Jimmie. "We have run into a bunch. People don't like a dusty road like this. In a few minutes, there won't be a car in sight, ahead or behind. You wait."

So I slacked still more, and jogged along. But, whizzing and rattling, car after car came rushing from behind and, as far as I could see in the reverse mirror, cars were following.

"There aren't any back roads any more in this world, Jim," I informed him. "All roads are main roads."

"Do you want to turn back and get on the pavement again, then?" demanded Jim.

"One's as bad as the other at this time of night," I informed him sadly. There was grit in our teeth already and the windshield had begun to go gray.

"Everybody told me this was a swell way to go home," said Jim. "Maybe they meant earlier in the season before everybody got fed up with the jam on the main highway."

I said nothing. I just took to the side of the road and held it at a nice 40, while with regular monotony cars from behind overtook us, blew their horns indignantly at my dust cloud and speeded furiously through, leaving a specially dirty dust cloud for me to hang in for two or three minutes.

"Nice, friendly people," I remarked.

But now even Jim was silent, huddled down with lips set grimly against the dust and his eyes squinted.

"We're overtaking somebody," I informed him suddenly.

Ahead, through the dust, I could see a car, then several cars.

"Don't tell me," I protested, "that there is a jam on this road too."

We came up in rear of a line of a dozen cars, all crowding and jostling close to each other.

"It's a detour," said Jim, who had stood up to look.

And it was a detour. Across the gravel highway barricades were set, fending us off to right and left, down traffic taking a narrow dirt road around a concession to the right, and up traffic apparently using a concession to the left.

"Well, sir," I said happily, "if there is anything else to recommend this road, I wish you'd mention it right now."

"How did I know it would be like this?" retorted Jim angrily.

"You didn't know anything about it—that's the trouble," I informed him.

And slowly taking our turn, while behind us fresh cars came furiously and dustily to a surprised stop, we turned off on to the side road which was baked hard and full of ruts and bumps and hummocks of dead grass.

"What are they doing?" I shouted to the man minding the barricade.

"They're improving it," he called back politely.

"Oh, goodie," I told him.

And as we lolloped and swayed and bumped along the narrow road with a slow and laboring string of cars ahead of us, I developed the theme.

"They're improving this road," I explained, "to relieve the main highway. They will pave it. So that instead of only one big traffic jam every Sunday night, you can choose between two big traffic jams."

"In that case," said Jim, "you'll have to adapt yourself to the 20th century. You'll have to modernize yourself."

"I think I'll give up motoring," I announced. "Motoring is getting too vulgar. The high-class thing to do presently will be never to motor."

"If you weren't so silly about traffic," said Jim, "we would have been spared all this bouncing around in the dust. We'd be somewhere outside the city limits right now, a couple of traffic bounders taking a little fun out of zig-zagging through the jam."

"I much prefer this," I said, even though we at the moment nearly crashed a spring in a hole in the dirt road, "to being in that main highway tangle. This may be a little rough and dusty; but it's safe."

And then a tire somewhere amongst us went bang and whined.

"Oh, ho," I said, brightly, "some poor beggar has got a blow out."

"It's us," advised Jim, hollowly.

And it was so.

"Pull as far off the road as you can," said Jim. "We have to let traffic past somehow."

So we came a few yards farther on, to a farm lane where we pulled out of the traffic and set the jack up on a wobbly turf and got all dusty taking off the spare and all greasy taking off the old one and all grass-stained putting on the new one and all wet with perspiration trying to release the jack so that it would come down.

And when we tried to get back out of the farmer's lane into the road, it was getting dusk and everybody was grim and angry and tired so that we had to wait until about 30 cars passed before there was a slight gap in the traffic. And when we did pop out into the road, the man we popped ahead of was so indignant that he blasted his horn for 10 seconds at us and came up right against our back bumper and we could hear him yelling things at us, but we could not hear the words.

And the whole thing was in a lovely holiday mood and very unlike the Sabbath altogether.

Working Party

May 20, 1939

"Trouble never ends," sighed Jimmie Frise.

"What's gone wrong now?" I sympathized.

"You know that swell wharf I built at the cottage last summer?" said Jim. "One of the neighbors was up at the Point last weekend and he tells me the whole thing is wrecked."

"How?" I demanded indignantly, for hadn't I helped

Jimmie talk about that wharf all the winter before last?

"The ice," said Jim. "The break-up of the ice in the spring. It just wrecked the whole thing. Bust the cribs and scattered the stones all over. Twisted the planks. A lot of them washed away and were lost."

"Ice is powerful," I agreed.

"My neighbor figures," said Jim, "it will cost about $50 to have the thing repaired. There's never any end, is there? Just when you think you've got level with the game, something turns up."

"How much did the wharf cost in the first place?" I asked.

So we carried one log, and, as we came up the bank, we could see Vic reclining in the sun and Skipper and Bumpy with a deck of cards out.

"Fifty dollars," said Jim. "But up in Muskoka, it's all the same. Building a new wharf or repairing a busted one, it's $50."

"Don't be silly," I protested. "You can get some of the local men to repair it for $10."

"No," said Jim, "up in the summer cottage belt it's different. They don't figure it by the hour or the material. They have a price for a job. A wharf costs $50. It doesn't matter what kind of a wharf it is. Any wharf is $50. Sometimes you get the best of the deal, sometimes the local man gets the best of it. But on the average it works out about fifty-fifty."

"Why don't you get the man that built this one and tell him the job wasn't strong enough?" I demanded.

"Docks are always built," explained Jim, "with the understanding that natural forces don't count. No, I know my Muskoka. There is nothing for it. I'll be stuck 50 bucks."

"How badly ruined is it?" I inquired.

"One of the end cribs," said Jim, "is entirely wiped out, the logs all gone and the stones strewn all over the place. The planking is ripped off, some of it is under water and some of it sticks up in the air. It's a mess."

"Why not wait until you go up in July before you spend any dough on it?" I suggested. "Fifty dollars next July doesn't look half as bad as $50 right now."

"A couple of good windy days," said Jim, "and my neighbor says the whole thing will be strewn along the shore for miles. I'm going to write up to the boys tonight and tell them to go ahead and mend it. A summer cottage without a good wharf is like a house without a garage."

"I was just thinking, Jim," I submitted. "What is there to repairing a dock? Building a dock, I agree, is something requiring knowledge and experience. But mending a wharf should be largely a matter of lifting and heaving."

"I can see you lifting 40-pound rocks to put in the crib," smiled Jim gratefully.

"I wasn't thinking of me," I smiled back very wily. "I was thinking of Skipper and Vic and Bumpy. Big, strong, athletic birds. Always wasting their strength on golf and squash racquets and climbing hills on fishing trips."

"Aaaaah," said Jim, lifting his eyebrows.

"I'll Co-ordinate the Work"

"How would this work?" I submitted eagerly. "Invite the whole gang of us up for a fishing weekend. The trout will be just at their best next week. There's some real good fishing at Port Sydney and other places less than 10 miles from your cottage. A fishing weekend. And no expense except the grub, which we will take with us, and do our own cooking. It will appeal to them. A lovely cheap weekend after trout at Jimmie's cottage."

"Then what?" asked Jim cautiously.

"When we arrive," I dramatized, "there will be your wharf, all bust. You'll see it first and be heartbroken. Everybody will sympathize with you. All our high spirits and excitement at arriving at the cottage will be dampened by the sight of you standing staring at your wrecked wharf, see? You can't get it out of your head. You'll walk down and stand dejectedly looking at it while we are busy carrying the luggage up to the house. I'll call the attention of the boys to you. You'll come up and stand around with a woebegone air."

"Then?" urged Jim.

"Why," I cried, "I'll assure you it's nothing. That the gang of us can put it right in an hour's work."

"It will take more than an hour," said Jim. "It might take a whole afternoon. We would have to drive logs down and make a new crib, fill the crib with rocks and spike down all the planks. It will be a messy job."

"Once we're at it," I assured, "we won't quit. Men like seeing things done."

"Not Bumpy and Vic," said Jim.

"Old Skipper will be the slave driver," I declared.

"And what will you be?" asked Jim.

"I'll be the foreman," I submitted. "I'll coordinate the work. Naturally, nobody expects a man of my size to lift big rocks, and nobody would want to be on the other end of carrying a log with me. I'm too short for that kind of work. It is my size that drove me into brain work."

"I haven't much hope of the bunch of you giving me much help," said Jim. "It seems to me I would be letting myself in for a lot of hard work while you all went fishing."

"Don't you want to save $50?" I demanded. "And if you can save $50 by merely using the help of a few hearty and athletic fishing partners who are guests at your summer cottage—"

"I suppose there's no harm," mused Jim. "After all, if they don't want to help—"

"Jim," I stated firmly, "you underestimate the nature of your friends. There is good in the worst of men. Just you start to work on that wharf and see how quick those birds will come to your aid."

"It seems a dirty trick," said Jim, "to invite them up for a fishing weekend and then run them into a lot of work."

"My dear man," I cried, "what's the difference between a fishing trip and a dock building trip? All a city man wants is a weekend in the open. A little exercise and fresh air. And in every man there is a love of constructing things. I know men who are addicted to wharf building. It's fascinating."

"Okay," said Jim, "we'll try it."

So we got on the telephone and called the gang up, it being only Monday; and framed up a weekend party. It was to be on the cheap. No expense. Jim would buy the provisions and we could divide it five ways, and that's all the expense we'd have outside the gas.

"They're all tickled to death," I pointed out to Jim. "A cottage weekend isn't to be sneezed at in times like these. Nobody has any money to throw away on expensive fishing trips."

"Or on busted docks," said Jim reflectively.

"That's it in a nutshell," I exclaimed. "In times like these people have a lot more heart than in piping times. You'll see. The boys will be tickled to death to put their backs into the job."

And Friday afternoon we all begged off work and met at Jim's and shifted all the luggage into two cars and so set off, in the high spirits of May, for Muskoka, which we reached in three hours, right at Jim's cottage.

Our entry was dramatic. My car being in the lead, I saw to that. The gate leading up from the shore road to the cottage is always a little rusty at the first of the season and it took a good minute to struggle with it, allowing the second car, with Jim in it, to catch up and stop behind us. Skipper had bailed out of my car and Bumpy and Vic piled out of the other, to stretch their legs.

"Good heavens," shouted Vic. "Look at the wharf."

And we all looked at the wharf. A long and heavy silence held us. In the silence Jim, very dramatically, took two or three hesitating paces forward and stood with his back to us silently regarding the ruin. His back was eloquent. A good actor can do more with his back than with his face. Jim's shoulders sagged.

"Aw, Jim," I said, deeply, "what a mess."

"The ice must have done it," said Skipper, the practical one.

"Boyoboyoboy," said Vic and Bumpy, sympathetically.

"That dock, boys," I submitted, "was brand new last season."

"I remember hearing you birds planning it all through the winter before last," said Skipper. "Why didn't you plan it right?"

"Could you have planned it better?" I demanded.

"Dock building is my specialty," said Skipper. "You ought to see the wharf at my place on the Kawarthas."

Jim had walked slowly and tragically down to stand and look closely at the wreckage.

"Then, Skipper," I said, "you're just the man Jim needs. Go on down and look the situation over while I get the stuff out of the cars and the cottage opened up."

I drove in the lane and Vic followed in his car and Bumpy came with us and we shifted the bags on to the veranda. We opened up the cottage and got the windows open, and had a quick look around to feel the mattresses and see which beds we'd choose. There is an art to arriving at a summer cottage weekend party.

By the time Jim and Skipper came up from the shore

we had a fire on and the lamps lighted against the evening that was falling. Jim had a long face and Skipper was detailing firmly just how you should slope a crib to stand against the strain and stress of the spring breakup of the ice.

"Cheer up, Jim," I shouted. Let's forget the wharf for tonight. Let's have a good supper and a pleasant evening, and we can see about the wharf tomorrow."

"I bet it will cost 75 bucks," groaned Jim.

"Pshaw, no," scoffed Skipper. "I bet it won't cost more than 50."

"How bad is it, Skipper?" I inquired, handling the frying pan full of eggs and bacon very skilfully. "Do you suppose we five might be able to make any sort of a repair job of it? After all. 50 bucks—"

The Excuses Begin

If I had four good men," said Skipper, "four good men, I said, who would obey my orders, I could have that wharf shipshape in one morning's smart work."

"Skipper," I cried, "you have four good men."

There is nothing I would rather do," announced Bumpy. "In fact, I love heaving things around. But only the middle of the week, my doctor went over me very carefully and told me to give up squash rackets for a while and to do no strenuous work of any kind for a period of two weeks, when he is going to give me another going over."

"There's a funny thing," exclaimed Vic. "I'm taking out some new insurance, and they found something a little wonky with my blood pressure. Just two days ago, that was. I have to come back in a week to have another test. So the doctor told me to lie around, this week, and get all the sun I can. I figured on just taking sun baths this weekend."

"Hm," said I.

"Well do you want me to be refused insurance?" demanded Vic sharply.

"I just said hm," I protested.

"But I didn't like the way you said it," said Vic.

"I tell you what," said Bumpy. "Vic and I could stand

by and sort of oversee and direct."

"Let's leave the whole thing till the morning," I suggested hastily. "We can think it over better then. I hate to see Jim stuck in for $50 if the gang of us could mend the job in two or three hours' work. Light work. The rise of trout isn't until late in the afternoon tomorrow anyway. We won't gain anything by rushing off early."

"That's what I say," agreed Skipper. "Let's take the weekend easy."

By which time the eggs were plump and the bacon curly and the table set and we gathered around. Jim caught my eye several times during the festive hour, and his expression was melancholy.

After supper, the others washed the dishes and I went out to listen to the stars and the soft splash of the gentle wind on the lake. And then they started a poker game, which I do not play because it steals away so many minutes from the lovely night; and in good time we prepared for bed.

"I'll get a handful of kindling for the fire in the morning," announced Skipper going out.

In three minutes he was back, his handkerchief wrapped around his right hand, and an air of disgust.

"I've bashed my hand," he muttered.

"Your fishing hand?" cried Jim solicitously.

We examined it. It looked a little red and scraped, but not serious. I got out iodine and plastered it liberally and Skipper bade me get a bandage out of his kit and bind his hand up carefully.

"You can't trust these injuries in the country," said Skip. "Tetanus."

And so to bed.

With the lark and the robins and small shrill redstarts and monotonous wrens, we woke and breakfasted, Skipper wearing his injured hand in his lapels, a la Napoleon, Bumpy complaining of a rather smothery feeling during the night and Vic confessing to a little migraine due, he feared, to some slight sinus trouble he had been reading about in a medical journal he had been reading while in the insurance company doctor's waiting room.

After the breakfast dishes were done there was a general unpacking of rods and fishing tackle on the sunny veranda, and Jim caught me inside the cottage to say: "I guess we'd better pass the wharf thing up."

"Let's make one try," I said. "Let you and me go down with a great show of purpose, and if none of them take the hint, we'll pass it up."

So we rolled up our sleeves and burst on to the veranda very purposeful.

"Just settle yourselves for a while, boys," I said heartily, "while Jim and I go down and see what can be done about the wharf."

"Do you want me, in an advisory capacity?" asked Skipper, holding up his bandaged hand.

"No, no, Skipper," we assured him kindly. It wasn't advice the situation called for.

So Jim and I went down and looked at the relic of the wharf in the quiet morning water. There really wasn't a great deal wrong with it, as a matter of fact.

"When you see it close," I pointed out, "all it needs is a couple of logs spiked on to that crib, and refill it with stones."

"These planks," said Jim, "can be all relaid and spiked in an hour."

"Let's start with the logs for the crib," I urged. "There's two of them on the beach, spikes and all."

So we carried one log, and as we came up the bank, we could see Vic reclining in the sun and Skipper and Bumpy with a deck of cards out, beginning a game.

"Pssst," I said, halting. "Listen? Isn't that a McGillivray's Warbler?"

"A what?" said Jim.

"Listen," I hissed, "that bird. That song, the clear, staccato notes . . ."

I laid the end of the log down and tiptoed into the grove east of the cottage, peering up into the trees to see this rare bird.

I was gone a little while, perhaps a little longer than that, because a bird lover loses all sense of time. It wasn't a McGillivray's Warbler, it was just a Myrtle, a very common warbler. But I heard the car horns calling and I returned out of the woods to find them all loaded and ready to go fishing; which we did, and had a grand day at Port Sydney. Skipper, even with his injured hand, casting best and catching 14 trout, including the biggest one a pound and 10 ounces, and everybody very happy and completely exhausted after a long day floundering and stumbling and toiling in the icy wild waters of the Muskoka River.

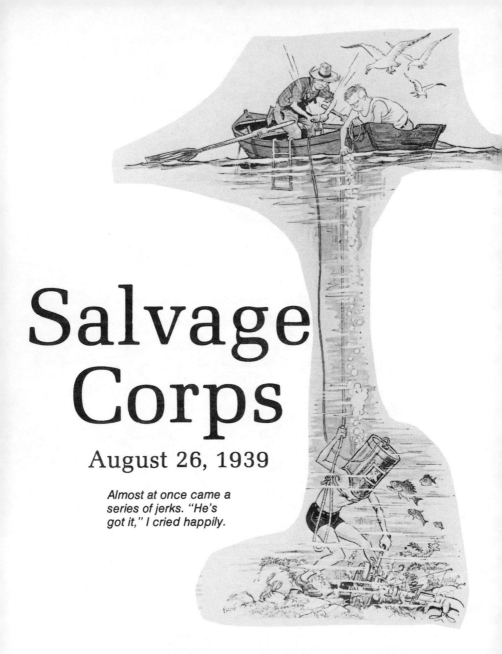

Salvage
Corps

August 26, 1939

Almost at once came a series of jerks. "He's got it," I cried happily.

"How the dickens," demanded Jimmie Frise hotly, "did you lose the engine?"

"It just fell off," I stated patiently.

"Outboard engines can't fall off," declared Jim loudly. "If you fasten the screws tight, and look at them once a day. Just once a day. It isn't much to ask."

182

"I am not the kind of man," I said, "who can look at anything regularly once a day. I'm the kind that fastens things once and for all. And if they don't hold, it's just too bad."

"It sure is too bad," said Jim. "Here I've been counting on borrowing your engine all week. I've planned this trip and got everything packed, the lunch hamper and everything. And now you say, quite coolly, your engine fell off."

"Well, it did," I stated hotly myself. "Do you imagine I pushed it off, just because you wanted to borrow it today? An engine that cost $140?"

"You take the loss of it very coolly," said Jim.

"Well, how else can you take it?" I retorted. "There I was sailing along, with a good old faithful engine humming behind me. And all of a sudden, plop, it's gone."

"Didn't you try to catch it?" demanded Jimmie.

"Catch it?" I cried. "I had hold of it. I was steering it. And it simply yanked itself out of my hand."

"But you could have made a grab for it," complained Jim.

"Listen, it was my engine, wasn't it?" I said angrily. "It wasn't your engine. Of course I made a grab for it. But it went straight down, leaving a trail of bubbles, and there I was, drifting along without even any oars."

"I think you were very careless," said Jim, "with something worth $140."

With people like Jimmie, it is useless to explain, much less argue. They get an idea in their heads and there it lodges.

"Jim," I said, "that engine didn't owe me anything. It was four years old and had done a good $140 worth of work for me. I don't regret its loss."

"You could have turned it in on a new one and got $40 for it," said Jim.

"I admit I am out some cash," I agreed. "But that isn't my philosophy. My philosophy is, what's to be is to be. I even agree that I should be the kind of man who carefully examines the screws on an outboard engine every day, so as to never lose that $40 turn-in value. But it so happens, I am the kind of guy that likes to pay $40 in four years just for the privilege of not having to look at the screws every day. That comes to only $10 a year. It isn't much to pay for a nice little bit of freedom."

"You'll never amount to anything, with that kind of a philosophy," stated Jim.

"Well, what do I want to amount to?" I inquired. "Do I want to amount to one of those tight, measly, mean old buzzards that go through life peering and prying at the screws of an outboard engine, so that he can be the richest guy in the graveyard?"

"I still think you might have taken a little precaution," said Jim, "especially when you knew I wanted that engine for today."

"Okay," I said. "Okay, okay."

"Whereabouts did it fall off?" inquired Jimmie.

"In 15 feet of water," I said, "right off that point by Bain's Island. It's a goner."

Wesley the Scientist

"Would you know," pursued Jimmie, "just about where? How far out from the point? And how many yards east or west of the point?"

"I suppose," I said sweetly, "you are going to dive for it? It only weighs 40 pounds, and it is only in 15 feet of water, and you can't even swim, much less dive."

"I had an idea," said Jim.

"I suppose," I continued, "that you will row the boat, while I dive for it, maybe?"

"No, you're past all diving," said Jim, looking at me in the middle, and he is able to express much with his glance. "But down at the Landing there is a young fellow, one of the native sons, who has a sort of diving outfit."

"You'll never find it," I assured him. "I spent two hours peering down in the water and dragging with big fish hooks. It's probably lodged amongst rocks."

"This kid," said Jim, "has a home-made diving outfit. He made it himself. It has a big cylinder that fits over your head, with pads around your shoulders. It is weighted, and he has a hose running down to the headpiece, with an ordinary tire pump to shove the air down."

"He couldn't go 15 feet down," I scoffed.

"He charges 25 cents," said Jim, "to let you go down eight feet at the wharf at his place, and see the fish and all the eerie things on the bottom."

It's extremely dangerous," I declared. "Lots of kids have been drowned playing with amateur diving suits. They get tangled up in the ropes."

"Well, this boy never lets anybody else monkey with it," explained Jim. "He takes charge and watches every move. I'm going to see if he won't help me find your engine."

It's hopeless, Jim," I assured. "You'd need a scow and everything."

But when an hour later Jim returned in a boat with a scientific young man and a big iron diving helmet built out of scrap iron, with a whole tackle of hose, pump, ropes and gadgets, they had no scow. The whole outfit was accommodated in an ordinary skiff.

"You pay the costs," said Jim, "if I get your engine."

"You won't get the engine," I said. "It's your adventure. How much is it?"

"Fifty cents an hour," said Jim. "Okay then; I'll pay the cost, and if I get the engine it will be mine."

"Nothing doing," I stated firmly. "That's my engine, even if it is at the bottom of the lake. If you want to go and get it, in order to go on this picnic of yours, okay. But it's my engine."

"Very well," said Jim, "I'll pay the costs, but I'll feel a lot freer about borrowing the engine any time I want it."

"I don't see how you could feel any freer than you do," I stated, getting into the boat with them.

The young man's name was Wesley, a name I had thought had gone out of fashion. He was extremely solemn about his diving apparatus. He had it as neatly coiled and stacked as if it were government property.

"The principle of the thing," he said, "is, Mr. Frise puts the helmet on and sets it snug and lowers himself over this little portable ladder I constructed. You hold the rope and pay it out as he descends. I am pumping.

We got to be very watchful the rope and the hose don't get snarled, or else."

Owing to Specific Gravity

"How does he get back up?" I inquired.

"Owing to specific gravity," said Wesley, "he is very light in the water. All he has got to do is sort of wish to come up and he gets light, see."

"And where does the air go you pump down?" I demanded.

"It just comes up in bubbles," said Wesley.

So we rowed across to Bain's Island, and I did a job of navigation. It is not easy to recollect details of your position after the lapse of a whole day, especially when, at the time of the disaster, you were filled with indignation, excitement and no oars in the boat. However, I had Wesley row slowly back and forward, searching my memory and watching the gooseflesh sprout all over Jimmie as he sat with increasing mock cheerfulness in his bathing suit, carefully feeling the iron helmet and the rubber hose and other parts of the machine.

"I think," I stated finally, "it was just right about here."

"Do we take soundings first?" asked Jimmie.

"Generally we do," said Wesley, and he took a clothesline with a stone on it and lowered it to the bottom. Then he hauled up, measuring it off in yards against his nose, arm extended.

"Seventeen feet," said he. "Nigh three fathoms."

"Are there any leeches around here?" asked Jimmie. "Or snapping turtles or anything?"

"No, I assured him. "This is fine clear water, though we did have quite a pest of watersnakes around Bain's Island last summer."

"Don't we anchor?" suggested Jim, seeing no anchor in the boat.

"No, you act as an anchor," said Wesley, "and you can walk along the bottom if you like."

"What are the signals?" asked Jim.

"Mr. Clark holds the signal rope," explained Wesley.

"One means okay, two means less air, three means pull me up."

Jim repeated these signals three times very loudly, and then swung on to the ladder that Wesley had hung overside. After a long last look at the coiled hose, the rope, which I held anxiously in my hand, and a final repetition of the signal numbers, Jim signalled Wesley to put the helmet on. It weighed Jim down, so heavy was it. Yet when he swung down and had the helmet half submerged he smiled cheerfully through the glass at us and moved his head around to show he was perfectly comfortable.

With a mute wave of his hand, he let go the ladder and I felt his weight on the rope. He weighed about 30 pounds, it seemed.

It was a grisly sort of feeling, paying out that rope with your friend tied to it. The rope was tied to a belt around Jim's chest, and a feeling of tremendous responsibility brought perspiration out all over me.

It was spooky, too, to see the continuous bubbles rising as Wesley slowly and anxiously pumped. But spookiest of all was to feel the boat being towed, via the rope in my hands, as Jim started to walk slowly around on the bottom.

He kept giving the one short jerk which meant okay.

"He's okay," I kept saying breathlessly to Wesley.

"Don't pay out the rope," commanded Wesley, the scientist. "Just let him have enough to tow us."

Jim walked this way and that. He seemed to climb over small hills and go down into little valleys. He probably wasn't down two minutes, but it seemed like an hour when he finally signalled three.

"Up," I said, rising and starting to haul.

"Up," echoed Wesley, very scientific, pumping with one hand and gently lifting the hose in with the other, coiling it.

And with a great bubble and burst, out came Jim's helmet beside the ladder and behind the steamy glass Jim was beaming.

"He's got it." I shouted.

"I See Something Shining"

Wesley hoisted the heavy helmet off, and Jim, all warm, breathed the cool air and then gasped: "I see something shining about 50 feet to the north there."

"It couldn't be that far out," I protested. "This is about where it fell off."

"Of course," agreed Jim. "But all I'm doing is looking on the bottom."

So Wesley rowed over in the direction Jim indicated, and again Jim went overside and again vanished into 16 feet of water, and Wesley and I, a little more courageously this time, manned the pump and the signal rope.

"Okay," came the signal and Jim hit bottom. And then almost at once came a series of sharp single jerks, okay, okay, okay.

"He's got it," I cried happily.

"You'll need to lift pretty easy," said Wesley. "He'll have his hands full."

Jim seemed to cruise around the bottom quite a bit, returning to the same place each time, and finally, after all of three minutes punctuated with seemingly joyous single jerks that all was well, Jim gave the three jerks to hoist. And as I hoisted, I knew the engine was with him.

Out of the water burst the round bell of the helmet. Through the steamy glass Jim beamed and shouted soundlessly.

Then out of the water came the propeller end of an engine.

But it was not mine.

It was a bigger, much newer engine than mine. It showed some signs of having been in the water a considerable time.

But in addition to the engine up flopped a steel fishing rod and reel, which Jim had tied by its line to the engine. Various other gadgets appeared, as I let go the rope and grabbed the engine to help hoist it on board. A wet sack of tools, a square brown tackle box, a heavy Thermos jar still full of something.

Wesley hoisted the helmet off Jim.

"Salvage," cried Jim breathlessly.

"This isn't my engine," I accused.

"No, and I saw no signs of yours," replied Jim. "But I found this one, and it's mine."

"And all the tackle," I complained.

"That," said Wesley, "must be the outfit those American tourists lost when they dumped here early in the season. They dragged all day for it and then gave it up."

"Did they leave any address?" asked Jim.

"No, they were just passers-by," said Wesley. "I guess this is all yours."

"But look here," I interrupted. "How about my engine?"

"Ask Wesley," suggested Jim, turning to inspect his beautiful big engine.

"How about continuing right now," I said. "I'll pay the costs."

"You can go down," said Jim. "I'm too cold."

He was blue. There were two leeches on him. He was shaking like a dog on a doorstep.

"Wesley," I suggested, "how much would you charge to get a friend and spend a day finding my engine here?"

"Fifty cents an hour, and a dollar an hour for my friend who goes down," said Wesley.

So tomorrow Wesley and his friend and I will continue the search for my engine. I know exactly where I lost it. It was about 100 feet this way of where we looked today. It is a wonder to me Jimmie did not see it shining.

Anyway, he's gone on his picnic, with his new engine.

Hare Raising

September 2, 1939

*"Get out of this,"
shouted the gentleman
angrily. "And keep out.
This is twice you have
done this."*

"I'm in a fix," said Jimmie Frise. "The rabbit has escaped."

"You should thank heaven," I submitted. "It was getting too big. In a few weeks you would have had to rent a ranch."

"You don't understand," said Jim. "It has escaped. But it is hanging around the neighborhood, digging up gardens, eating verbenas and choice cannas. The whole block is up in arms."

"You should worry," I offered. "Good riddance. Just tell your boy that it ran away because it was lonesome for him when he went away to the cottage."

"The kid wanted to take him to the cottage," said Jim. "I wish I had let him. It would have been the best solution. He would have escaped up there in the wilds, where he belonged."

"Will you ever forget the night we got him?" I recalled. "In April. We were up looking over the trout stream. On the way home, just south of Glenlivet, we saw him in the headlights of the car, crouched on the gravel road."

"He looked awfully cute and tiny then," sighed Jim. "You never would have believed what a fiend he would turn out."

"You pulled the car up," I recollected. "And sneaked out, leaving the headlights full on blinding him. And, with a squeak, he was in your grasp. I cuddled him all the way home."

"You wanted to toss me for him," sighed Jim. "I wish I hadn't been so possessive."

"He has been a great pet for your kid," I consoled. "I'm afraid the boy will be heartbroken to think you let him escape. I bet he's looking forward to seeing the rabbit more than he is to starting to school."

"A wild thing never makes a real pet," stated Jim. "It's a big mistake ever to capture a wild thing for a pet."

"I never saw a cuter creature," I declared, "than that rabbit during May and June. He grew so gangly and long-legged. And in his eyes, such an expression of mischief and cunning. You never see tame rabbits like him. Anyway, he wasn't a rabbit; he was a hare. A European hare."

"He was a jack rabbit," said Jim.

"No, that's a mistake," I informed him. "These great big so-called jack rabbits that are over-running Ontario aren't rabbits and certainly aren't jack rabbits. The jack rabbit is a hare that belongs in Texas and the southwestern states, and it is only half the size of these Ontario beasts."

"How did these get loose?" demanded Jim.

"In 1915," I advised, "a man had about 50 European hares in a pen somewhere down around Brantford. A flood set them free and they have spread all over. He had imported them from England to breed as a food supply during the war. They are the common wild hare of Europe. They don't grow so big in England as they do here. We get them up to nearly 20 pounds."

The Neighbors Protest

"This Itsy-Bitsy of ours," said Jim, "weighed 12 pounds, I'll bet, before he got away. I bet he weighs more now. Eating cannas and prize dahlias and everything. Boy, am I in for trouble? One of the neighbors has warned me that he is going to sue me for the loss of his prize dahlias. He said he paid $50 for his dahlias and now he can prove my rabbit ate them."

"It isn't your rabbit now," I protested.

"Yes," sighed Jim. "I asked my lawyer. He says that even if a pet escapes, it is still your pet. If you import a tiger into the community, it is your tiger, whether in its cage or out of it."

"Itsy-Bitsy is no tiger," I argued. "He looks like Pan. He looks like some wild god. But he certainly wouldn't hurt a flea."

"He wouldn't?" cried Jim. "I wish you'd come around after supper and see some of the things he's done. He fairly kicks a garden to pieces. He bites ornamental bushes. He digs up bulbs and eats a whole row of asters. A helenium bush is just a snack to him. Come around after supper and I'll show you some of his jobs."

"Have you seen him since he got away?" I inquired.

"Everybody's seen him, but me," said Jim. "I only wish I could spot him, just once. I'd fix him."

"You wouldn't hurt your child's pet?" I cried.

"Pet?" said Jim. "I'll pet him. I've sat for the last three nights with a shotgun in my garden."

"You can't shoot a gun inside the city," I protested.

"Just once," said Jim, grimly. "Just one bang, and before anybody could figure out what it was it would never happen again. A mystery."

"The law is the law," I assured.

"Listen," said Jim. "When I brought that rabbit home we kept it in a little wooden box with screen on top. In less than a week, after feeding it lettuce and cabbage until the grocery bill went up two dollars a week, I had to build a pen. You remember that first pen?"

"The last one I saw you building," I reminded, "you had to bury the wire fence two feet down in the ground."

"I had to build a bear cage for it," grated Jim. "We fed it cabbage and lettuce and scraps. Then we noticed that if we threw lamb chop bones in, they disappeared, too."

"Oh, come," I begged.

"Yes, sir," said Jim. "Somebody threw in scraps of meat and stuff by mistake, and Itsy-Bitsy ate them all. Why, a week ago, before he escaped; I would save time by tossing a can of bully beef into his pen, and he'd kick the can around until it burst open. You never saw so savage a beast. The way he'd guzzle that bully beef. I think he even ate the cans."

"Aw, Jim," I protested.

"Well, anyway, I'm sore at him," submitted Jim. "He has let me in for a lot of trouble, and I'm afraid to go home at night for fear of a committee of neighbors waiting for me. He stays right inside the one block. He

193

makes the gardens of our own block his preserve. And, boy, he is ruining them. In three nights he has kicked, dug, scraped and eaten five lovely September gardens into wrecks."

A Rabbit Hunt in Town

"Why don't you lure him back?" I asked. "And then you could take him for a ride into the country and let him go up near Glenlivet."

"Haven't I tried?" cried Jim. "The night he got loose, my next door neighbor's zinnia bed was wrecked as if by a cyclone. So I filled his pen with lettuce, cabbages and everything nice I could think of, and then sat up in the moonlight until midnight, with a string on the door of the pen."

"And he didn't come?" I asked.

"In the morning the neighbor on the other side had a 20-foot bed of cannas ripped to pieces."

"How can they prove it's your rabbit?" I asked.

"They've seen him in the act," confessed Jim. "And, anyway, you know the neighbors' attitude towards any kind of a pet."

"Let them holler," I suggested.

"One of them," said Jim, "has sent me a lawyer's letter, threatening to sue me. Others have telephoned warnings. Last night I went out in the garden and everybody that was out in theirs went right indoors as soon as they saw me."

"I won't see any friend of mine stuck," I declared. "Jim, I'll help you. I have the solution."

"What?" inquired Jim eagerly.

"We'll borrow Joe Shirk's hounds," I said, "and stage a little rabbit hunt right in the city."

"Why didn't I think of that!" cried Jim.

"They're the best little hounds in York county," I submitted. "They'll have that old fat jack in less than three minutes."

"How silly," said Jim. "A dog. If there were a man-sized dog in the whole block, that rabbit would have been 10 miles from there by now. But old Rusty is up at the cottage with the family. And all the rest of them we have in the block are lap dogs and Scotties and other gherkin hounds."

"Itsy-Bitsy is as good as gone already," I said, very workmanlike. "Do you mind if they kill him?"

"I suppose they'll have to," said Jim. "I can't imagine them chasing him out of the city the way they would chase him out of a county. Too much traffic and everything."

"They'll move him out of your block anyway," I pointed out.

"And that's what counts," agreed Jim.

So we telephoned Joe Shirk and when we explained the situation to him he was delighted.

"A rabbit hunt in town?" he cried. "It's unique. I'll bring two or three of my best derbies."

And no time being like the present, we agreed that tonight was the night. Just about the quiet of sundown.

I was at Jim's when Joe arrived. In the back of the car, coupled together, he had three little hounds, derbies, as they call them in their first year of running. Lovely little open-marked beauties that yowled and bayed with excitement, as if they could smell Itsy-Bitsy already.

Joe took them on leash into the yard while we looked the situation over. It was a warm evening, but few of the neighbors seemed to be in their gardens. Jim showed Joe a couple of the neighbor gardens, all clawed up by the brutal rabbit. The hounds sniffed anxiously along the borders, emitting small whimpering sounds.

"Do we need clubs or anything?" Jim inquired, hefting a clothes prop.

"It'll be all over in a minute," assured Joe Shirk. "Confined in these gardens, the rabbit won't have a chance. The boys will have him and he'll never know what hit him."

"Good-by, Itsy-Bitsy," said Jim, not without sentiment.

"Hoy in there," gloated Joe Shirk, slipping the leashes off the little hounds.

And with a furious waggling and snorting, the hounds buried their noses and started scouring along the fence. Almost immediately, one of them vaulted the fence lightly, into the neighbor yard. And instantly his beautiful bugle voice broke into a glad acclaim.

"Tally-ho," shouted Joe Shirk, leaping the fence. "Gone awaaaaaaayy!"

And before we knew it, Jim and I were vaulting the fence too, while with a racket like 15 devils, the three little hounds took the line and vanished over the next wire fence.

Music of the Hounds

From back doors, people came popping. But it was too exciting behind those little hounds to waste time explaining. That could come later. Over five fences we leaped and climbed before we came to the end of the block and turned to race back up towards Jim's again.

"Easy, easy," shouted Jim as Joe vanished into a thick forest of beautiful late-blooming delphinium. But Joe was a master of hounds. Where hounds go, he would follow. The delphiniums, out of their season anyway, showed the signs of his passing.

Jim and I went round the end of the yard, just as a door opened and a furious voice roared at us. Windows were opening. Doors opening. A sense of excitement rising.

"Wait," gasped Jim, as we scrambled over a picket fence into a jungle of golden glow and salvia. "They're running in a circle. Let's wait here and cut him off."

Breathing heavily, we crouched in the jungle, peering out into the garden. Far off, we could hear the little hounds yelping furiously and Joe's voice as he heartily hie-ed them in. Then we heard them turn and start back down the inside of the block.

"They're about passing my place," whispered Jim. By now, many voices were shouting, both women and men.

The lovely riot of the hounds came nearer, turned, and started up towards us.

"Watch," hissed Jimmie.

And out of the perennial border we saw Itsy-Bitsy, fresh as a daisy and with a look of sport in his face, come lolloping, a good two gardens ahead of the ravening hounds.

196

"Git him," rasped Jim, as we both leaped towards Itsy-Bitsy.

But he bounded airily past us, as though we had been anchored, and when the hounds came crashing and blundering through, we joined them.

The next fence up, a lady and a gentleman were sitting in garden chairs, amidst their cannas, looking highly alert. When we came plunging through, they leaped up.

"Get out of this," shouted the gentleman angrily. "And keep out. This is twice you have done this."

But it went on more than twice. Itsy-Bitsy was too well fed. Jim and Joe and I quit the third time round and waited in Jim's garden while the hunt went round and round. Seven times they went the grand circle of the block, never quite the same route twice, but barging through different borders and beds each time. Jim just sat and groaned. The telephone rang indoors, but he ignored it. It rang and rang. Neighbors came and shouted across fences. But Jim just sat bowed, groaning, and I patted his shoulder and Joe Shirk stood transfixed with delight, listening to the music of his hounds, nodding his head and whispering to himself their names, and encouraging them with queer inaudible cries.

The eighth time round, Itsy-Bitsy must have got tired, for suddenly the music changed.

"They've gone out an alley," shouted Joe, rushing for the side entrance.

"Let them go," said Jim, brokenly.

And with Joe gone, we sat in the darkling evening, listening to the chase vanish into the next block, and the next and the next, farther and farther, until the music of the hounds was a whisper.

Then we went in and took the receiver off the telephone and let it lay, and sat down to compose a circular letter to all the neighbors in Jim's block. A letter of explanation and apology.

But all we have so far is:

"Dear Sir or Madam, as the case may be."

Up the tree I went heavily. "Stop," came a sharp voice. It was a strange voice.

Coon Hunt

September 23, 1939

"It's a pity," said Jimmie Frise, "there isn't more for a man to do at this season of the year."

"There's duck hunting," I informed him, "and in a few weeks there will be pheasant shooting. And then deer hunting."

"If our ancestors," said Jim, "hadn't slaughtered this country, September and October would be two of the merriest months of the whole year."

"How do you mean?" I demanded.

"To think," cried Jim, "that here in Canada, less than a century old, with vast areas still wild and unpopulated, we should have to import pheasants from China in order to supply something for us to shoot."

"Our forefathers had to civilize the country," I protested.

"Civilizing a country, I suppose," snorted Jim, "means killing everything in sight."

"I'm afraid I don't follow you," I submitted. "You wanted your ancestors to shoot less, so that you could shoot more. Is that it?"

"They might have left more than they did," said Jim. "But it strikes me as funny that we in Ontario, after one brief century, should have to import game birds from China, which has been settled for thousands of years."

"I guess we did go at settling Ontario a little furiously," I agreed.

"September and October," declared Jim, "are livelier months in Pennsylvania and Tennessee than they are in Ontario. And I mean sport."

"And they've been settled three hundred years," I agreed.

"There must be something funny about Ontario," mused Jim. "Why should we have to work so hard for our game here?"

"Largely because," I informed him, "a very large part of Ontario, all the unsettled part, the north country and the lake country, is all rock. It is not fertile."

"I've been reading lately," said Jim, "a good deal about the sport they have in states like Pennsylvania and Kentucky. They go in for sociable sports. Things that a dozen men can enjoy together. Like fox hunting at night, where they put their hounds out to chase a fox and the hunters, instead of chasing after the hounds on horses, or on foot with guns to shoot the fox, just sit in company around a big bonfire and listen to their hounds chasing the fox."

Trained Coon Hounds

"That's southern for you," I commented.

"Lazy and indolent. I like the chase."

"Then they have coon hunting," went on Jimmie. "That's got action. They have specially trained coon hounds."

"I love the music of hounds, day or night," I admitted.

"On a bright moonlight night," said Jim, "it must be

glorious. Away go the hounds, baying. And all the hunters follow after, armed with lanterns and potato bags."

"Potato bags?" I exclaimed.

"They don't kill the coon," said Jim. "After a wonderful chase, over fields, through woods, from one woodlot to another, over fences, across creeks, the coon leads the hounds until finally they overtake him and he goes up a tree."

"This sounds good." I agreed.

"The hunters following," explained Jim, "are by now straggled out, some trying to keep up with the hounds, others using their wits to take short cuts, employing their knowledge of the country, and of coons, to dope out where the coon is heading. When the coon trees, the hounds make a different sound, they 'bark treed,' as the saying is. Then all the hunters converge on that woodlot, and gather around the tree, build a big fire, their lanterns all gleaming, and they see the green shine of the coon's eyes as it stares down."

"How long does a chase last?" I asked.

"Sometimes half an hour, sometimes two or three hours, with a good big old coon," said Jim. "Then when all are gathered and the best men are there first, one man shinnies up the tree and shakes the coon down. The dogs pounce on it and before it is killed, the coon is put in the bag. They can either kill it for fur, keep it for a pet or let it go for another hunt after they have proved, back in town, their prowess."

"And the prowess of the hounds," I reminded.

"That's true," said Jim. "As the hunters follow the chase, they always pause, every few minutes, to hear whose hound is leading. When there is a check, they all stop dead still and listen to hear whose hound first finds the scent again."

"That ought to be grand fun," I confessed. "It's a wonder we don't follow that sport here."

"I can't understand it," said Jim. "There are plenty of coons, even in Old Ontario."

"Let's get Joe Shirk some night," I submitted, "and try it. He's got five hounds."

"There may be some perfectly good reason," said Jim,

"why we don't hunt coons in Ontario."

Exploring Recreation Field

"Well, we can find it out," I said firmly. "If there is some recreation we are overlooking in this province, Jim, it is our duty to discover it and report the facts to the public."

"Agreed," said Jim heartily. "I can think of no means of making a livelihood better than exploring the field of recreation for the benefit of the public."

"What this world needs," I assured him, "is more ways of amusing itself, not more ways of worrying."

So we telephoned Joe Shirk and when we outlined the proposition to him, he leaped at it. Joe is one of those men, now unhappily growing fewer in number, whose function in the scheme of nature is to breed hounds. Not setters or spaniels or lap dogs or any of the other of man's best friends; but plain hounds that sit about bored to death until turned loose after rabbit, fox, deer or other game. One thousand years ago, the Joe Shirks and their hounds were part of the essential economy of the human race. They were to the world what the big meat packers are to our present day economy. Without Joe Shirks and hounds, society did not eat.

"I'll bring the whole pack, said Joe. "And tonight ought to be the night, because the moon is just coming full."

Then Jim telephoned long distance to three of his country uncles and the third announced that he had at least two families of coons in his main bush lot.

"And," said Jim, hanging up the phone, "it's less than 50 miles from the city."

We tried to get together a party. We called up all our fishing friends, all our duck hunting acquaintances and all our deer shooters, but they were all engaged. It was too short notice. Some had dates for the movies with their wives. Others wanted to stay in because it was Thursday night and a big night on the radio. But when we picked Ed up in the car, it was just the three of us in the party, and after a brisk after-supper drive of one hour flat, we arrived at Jim's uncle's.

And even he couldn't come with us because "Four Feathers" was showing at the village theatre.

"One of the reasons why there isn't much sport in Ontario," declared Jimmie, "is that Ontario people aren't much interested in sport. That is, unless they can sit down to it. In grandstands."

"You won't get much sitting down tonight," said Joe Shirk. "These here hounds are raring."

As indeed they were. All the way out in the car, I had been in the back of the car with the five of them, and they had climbed and crawled and rubbed all over me, whining and shivering with uncontrolled excitement, until I smelt like a hound myself.

From Jim's uncle's, we drove around a concession so as to come on the back of the great bushlot that ran the full way across the concession, a nice swamp buried in its midst. The uncle had one small field of corn stooked, but on the back concession, a farmer had fifteen acres of it, and would most certainly welcome any coon hunters because the coons were playing havoc with the corn.

It was frosty and still and the wide moon just rising by the time we sided the car and let the hounds loose. In the dim first light of moon, the hounds scattered along the road, sniffing and very busy.

Over the meadow and up to the edge of the woods we walked, with lanterns unlighted, stumbling in the moonlight until we came to the edge of the great corn patch. The stooks rose spooky in the soft dark, and the hounds ran and investigated them eagerly.

"Do they know coons?" I asked Joe Shirk as we puffed along.

"They've never hunted coon," said Joe, but they'll investigate any trail. And if we show interest, they'll soon get wise and follow it."

Which proved the case. For suddenly, one hound halted and arched his back and began sniffing furiously at the ground. Another and then another hound instantly joined him, and with backs arched and tails waving, they followed the trail into the corn patch.

"Hie," called Joe Shirk in a low, excited voice after them, "hie in there, **Mike**. Hie in there, Sally. Hie, hie, hie!"

And from the midst of the stooked field there suddenly rang out the sound that echoes out of the ages in the hearts of all men in health. The deep, baleful bay of a hound. A sound like a trumpet, like a French horn, like an oboe, like certain of the nobler notes of a grand organ.

"We're away," shouted Joe Shirk vanishing into the cornfield. "Gone away. Awaaaay."

And all five hounds filled the moonlit night with a symphony of their doomlike wails and quavers.

"Light lanterns," commanded Jim breathlessly.

With shaking hands, we lit the lanterns—plain coal oil lanterns, Jim said, were essential implements of the chase when coon hunting. The hounds curved away and then, from the far end of the cornfield, swept back towards the woodlot.

"It may be an hour," cried Jim, leading off, "so save your wind."

Into the bushlot the cry went, and the whole township seemed to rock and shiver with the music of the hounds. We could see Joe Shirk's lantern bobbing away off in the bush, disappearing and reappearing.

"They're headed for the swamp," shouted Jim over his shoulder. "It's a big old hecoon."

He used a sort of Kentucky accent.

Into the bushlot we thrust, our lanterns waving. And if you want to get into a real tangle, try pushing through unfamiliar woods at night with an oil lantern.

Over logs, into thickets, around boulders, under rusty old lost wire fences, we plunged and labored. When Jim came to a sharp halt and cried—"Listen!"

The music of the hounds had changed from the rhythmic baying and was now a series of sharp barks followed by a high long drawn howl.

"Treed," cried Jim, "already!"

In 10 minutes of staggering, blundering, plunging and falling, we reached the spot where Joe Shirk had a fire lighted and was sitting back, filled with broad joy, watching his beloved hounds bounding and baying up the trunk of a tall tree.

Ceremoniously, we set our lanterns down and stood

around peering into the tree. The eyes of the coon were shining. But they were red, not green.

"Who climbs?" asked Joe Shirk.

But I had already wrapped one leg around the tree. For if there is anything I don't like, it is a mix-up with dogs snarling and snapping around on the ground. I don't want to be mistaken for any coon. It is more comfortable to watch such a scene from above.

Mistaken Identity

Up the tree I went, heavily.

"Stop," came a sharp voice.

It was a strange voice.

"What are you men doing here?" demanded a stranger advancing into the firelight.

"We've got a coon treed here," said Jim, heartily. "You're welcome to join us, mister."

"I'm the game warden," said the stranger sternly. "Don't you gents know it is illegal to hunt coons?"

"Illegal?" I asked, from away up in the tree.

"Coons are fur bearing animals," said the stranger. "You have to have a license to hunt them. They have to be hunted in season. And it is illegal to hunt at night."

Just ahead of me, on the branch, a dark shape loomed.

In spite more than anger, in spite to think of all the reasons we can't have fun in this world, I gave the branch a nasty twitch.

The dark shape scrambled for a hold but lost it, and fell with a thud to the ground.

The hounds, instead of staging the coon fight I expected, leaped back.

It was a porcupine.

So we all sat around the fire, game warden and all, and talked about the sport our grandfathers used to have in these parts.

Say Nothing and Saw Wood

"Two axe handles is the length of log I like," said the farmer. You would think he would have taken a turn at the saw. But not he.

November 25, 1939

"Canada," asserted Jimmie Frise, "is the most fortu-
nate land on earth."

"It has its defects," I agreed, "but in the main there is no country on earth so secure."

"It is part of the British Empire," enumerated Jim, "and its only neighbor, the United States, is the next strongest nation on earth."

"A friendly neighbor," I submitted, "who will always take the keenest interest in our affairs, if for no other reason than for her own safety."

"We can call upon either," stated Jimmie, "for anything we need. Money, men, materials. Whatever we want we can get from those two greatest and friendliest of nations. Yet we are free to do as we please. We can take their goods or refuse them. Accept their people or decline them. We have all the advantages and none of the disadvantages."

"You don't get anything for nothing, Jim," I interrupted. "I don't like to have all the advantages. We may be running up a very heavy bill."

"How could they collect?" demanded Jim.

"Well, for instance," I submitted, "suppose the United States decided that it needed all its gas and oil? Suppose it decided not to sell us any more oil, gas or hard coal?"

"We've got coal in Nova Scotia," said Jim, "and in the west. And we could buy our oil from Peru and Mexico and places."

"But still, just supposing," I offered. "Suppose the United States decided not to sell us any hard coal, oil or gas? My furnace is an oil furnace. Yours uses hard coal. It might take quite a few weeks to get the coal coming from the east and west. Maybe the American-owned oil wells in Peru and Mexico wouldn't have any to spare our boats."

"We could burn wood," said Jim. "It's a little more trouble, to keep stoking wood into a furnace. But still, we wouldn't freeze."

"It would be an awful nuisance," I submitted. "But I guess if our grandfathers got along with wood, so can we. And Canada has plenty of wood."

"The trouble with progress," declared Jim, "is that it makes us so helpless.

"That's a queer thing," I admitted.

"Yes, sir, the more we progress, as a society," went on Jim, "the more helpless we become individually. Each of us is given some little chore to do in the great march of progress. And the more perfect we become at our little chore, the more helpless we become as human beings. My grandfather, for example, was self-sustaining. He cut his own wood. He kept his own cows and hogs. His wife made most of his clothes, or could."

"Ah, or could," I arrested him. "That's the sticker. We still could cut wood."

It's Easy to Become Soft

"Could you milk a cow?" inquired Jim.

"No, you milk the cows and I'll cut the wood," I submitted.

"There you go," cried Jim. "Starting to progress and specialize right away."

"I bet I could milk a cow if I had to," I said. "Just because we've had a couple of generations of progress is no reason for imagining that we have lost all our talents."

"It's easy to become soft," said Jim. "But it's hard to grow hard again. You and I go camping. We keep alive the faint spark of our pioneer ancestors. But think of the tens of thousands of people right here in town who would be practically ruined if they had to go camping and live by it."

"I think," I said, suddenly, "I'll lay in a cord of wood or so."

"Aha," laughed Jim. "As soon as we speak of camping you think of chopping firewood. And as soon as you think of firewood, your mind leaps back to the thought of having to cut enough wood to keep your furnace going."

"You follow my train of thought," I agreed. "The way the world is, I think every city dweller ought to have a cord of good wood in his cellar."

"Look," said Jim enthusiastically, "what better way could we spend Saturday than going out and cutting down a tree?"

"I've got plans for Saturday," I stated. "My family has me all dated up."

"Pah," scoffed Jim, "you're always talking about your

pioneer ancestors, but at the slightest challenge from them, you scuttle to cover."

"I never scuttled in my life," I retorted. "I can carry a canoe over a portage as good as any of my ancestors, I can make a better camp fire than a lot of them, I bet; and since most of them were missionaries to the Indians and county clerks and that sort of thing, I bet I can shoot a rifle a lot better than they could."

"But you can't saw wood like they could," jeered Jim.

"For one thing, Mr. Frise," I countered, "where would you find a tree to cut down? There are no wild trees any more, anywhere. All the bush you can find within 50 miles of Toronto is privately owned woodlots. Even in the far north, somebody owns the timber rights to every stick that grows. You can't just go out and cut a tree down and bring it home."

"We could buy a tree," suggested Jim. "I bet any farmer would sell us a maple or a birch out of his woodlot for a dollar, if we were going to cut it."

"And he'd think us nuts, into the bargain," I agreed. "Jim, as long as society is organized, why not leave to those who cut wood the job of cutting wood, and we'll attend to the cartoons and the stories in the newspapers?"

"It was just a test I was suggesting," said Jim. "I agree you are a handy little gent with an axe around a camp, cutting a few armfuls of dead wood. But I wonder how you'd size up, say, with a good big hard maple with four cords of wood in it?"

"I've cut plenty besides dead wood," I declared.

"Then what are you scared of?" inquired Jim sweetly.

"I'm scared of nothing," I informed him. "I say my family has me all dated up this Saturday."

A Thinker on a Fence

But there is a sort of way Jimmie has of just sitting there with a superior smile on his face that cuts right to the bone. It is more forceful than any argument. And that is why, after lunch Saturday, we both were in the car heading rural, all dressed up in our woodsmen's clothes which we had put away until next fishing season.

We also had an axe which I borrowed from a neighbor who goes in for good tools; and Jimmie had borrowed a crosscut saw from a cousin of his who had only recently moved in from the farm, with all his goods and chattels, to take up the easy city life.

We drove north of Toronto about 30 miles until we saw far to the east a large area of bush. We took roads that led us, by concessions, into this area where woodlots grew larger and larger and the fields smaller. It was one of those stony bits of country that jut down out of the north into Ontario's best agricultural area.

We drove slowly along the sideroads, through the bushlots, looking for a farmhouse that had a good big woods, with a nice-sized maple or birch tree handy to the fence and not too much surrounded by other trees. We wanted, so to speak, a lone maple in the middle of a field, near the fence.

"We can cut it down," said Jim, "saw it into logs by dark. And then come back next Saturday and chop it."

And there, at a turn of the road, was the ideal trees, in the ideal field, and instead of an ideal farmhouse, nearby, if there wasn't the farmer sitting on the rail fence right near the tree.

"It's an omen," I cried. "It couldn't be more perfect."

For the tree, tall and sound, stood amidst light brush so that it would be easy to fall without a lot of complications.

"How would you like to sell that tree?" I called smilingly out of the car window as we drew level with the farmer.

He looked a little surprised and then cast a calculating eye on the tree.

"Sell a tree?" he asked genially. He had a most interesting face. A strong, thinking face. It was as if we had interrupted him sitting there on the fence thinking deep thoughts.

"Yes, sir, that tree," I said, getting out of the car and walking over to him. "You see, we live in the city. We wanted a cord of wood each in our cellars. And it occurred to us that since our grandfathers always sawed their own wood, it might be an interesting experiment to

211

see if we were still capable of doing the same."

The farmer studied us with amused interest.

"The war," he hazarded, "is turning a lot of you city toilers back towards the land."

"It's a fact," we admitted.

He turned and studied the tree.

"We'd pay you whatever you think the tree's worth," said Jim. "A dollar or so?"

"It has always seemed to me," said the farmer, "that if a man had the energy and the will to cut a tree down and cut it into wood, he had a right to the tree."

"Ah, but property," I reminded him. "What about the rights of property?"

"True," reflected the farmer, sitting easy on the rail fence, "but property has limits. There stands a tree. And there stand two men willing and eager to chop it down. Which is the greater property? The tree or the will to convert it, by labor, into something useful?"

"You're quite a Socialist," admired Jim.

"Yes," said the farmer reflectively, "a man gets a lot of time to think, out here in the country."

A Sentimental Contact

"Well, how about it?" I asked very businesslike. "Can we have the tree? And how much?"

"As far as I am concerned," said the farmer, "the tree is yours, and all I want out of it is the pleasure of sitting on this here fence and seeing two city men finding out if they're as good as their grandfathers."

So we all laughed, and Jim and I went and got the axe and saw out of the car, and the farmer made himself comfortable on the fence.

"You might check up on our technique," suggested Jim. "My friend here says he comes of a long line of tree choppers.

First we cleared away the brush to give the axe and saw plenty of room. Then we studied the lay of the land, the slope of the tree itself and the place we would like to fell the tree.

"Now," I announced, "first I chop a large nick in this

side of the tree, which is the direction we want it to fall."

And freeing my braces and rolling up my sleeves, spitting on my hands and bracing my feet wide apart, I started to swing the three-pound axe. Maple is tough wood. It is springy and slick, but tough. I took little chips and then larger ones, and the farmer on the fence kept up a quiet commentary, advising me to avoid masticating or chewing the tree, in the beaver tradition, and to lay the axe into the wood so as to spring a large, clean chip. He also amused us, as time fled, with various views he had on life and property, on the changing times, on communism and socialism and the need of ever-increasing understanding between those who owned the means of production and those who used them.

After quite a long time, I got a fair-to-middling nick on the low side of the tree. Then Jim took the axe and started the other nick on the upper side, a little higher than the first nick. And when he got it fairly deep, we took the crosscut saw and sawed through quite a way. We were pretty tired by now, and went and sat on the fence for a few minutes with the farmer. But he said we were doing fine, even if our grandfathers had moved into the city. And he didn't offer to help us with the increasingly ticklish job of sawing towards the lower and larger nick.

"I think if you use the axe from now on," he suggested at last.

So working on the larger nick, Jim and I, by turns, deepened and widened the lower nick. We must have been an hour and a half at it. But, of course, we weren't working on a time schedule. We were merely making a sentimental contact with the past.

At last, a creak warned us that our tree was beginning to feel the loss of balance. Very cautiously, ready to leap back at the first sign of sway, we swung the axe bite by bite, examining, checking and swinging with deliberation. And all at once, with a slight cracking sound, the great tree started its plunge; a rushing sound grew; Jim and I fled well back of the stump, and down came our firewood.

For some minutes we studied the fallen monarch in triumph, a much larger tree lying than standing. We spent half an hour chipping off the branches and top. And then we measured off two axe handles and started to saw our first log.

"Two axe handles is the length of log I like," said the farmer, still sitting on the fence though the afternoon was waning and the wind becoming chill. You would think he might have warmed himself with a turn at the saw. But not he.

We got the first log nicely sawed and the farmer gave us a rousing cheer for our workmanlike job when over the hill came a stranger, who, when he saw us, hurried.

"Well, well, well," said the stranger, a fat man in overalls. "What's doing here?"

The other farmer had got off the fence and was standing on the far side.

"Well, sir," we replied, glad of the rest, "we're a couple of Toronto men who have just acquired a tree and are cutting it up for firewood."

"Acquired?" said the stranger with interest.

"Yes, this gentleman gave us the tree," explained Jim. "Very kindly, too. He made the interesting proposition that if a man had the energy to cut a tree up, the tree ought to be his."

The stranger laughed.

"Unfortunately," said he, "it isn't his tree. It's mine. He's my hired man, and he's a little gone in the head. A little simple, as you doubtless realize."

He said this right in front of the other man.

"But we've cut it," we began, "we've done a lot of work. How much do you want for the tree . . . ?"

"I won't sell it," said the farmer. "I need it myself. I sent this lad down after lunch to cut it and chop it up for me."

"But look here," we said, "how were we to know . . . ?"

"Now, now," said the farmer, "you could tell by the talk of him that he wasn't all there. He's some kind of a Socialist or something. And anyway, does it stand to reason that anybody would give anything away for nothing?

214

Gentlemen, don't tell me, you city men, that you would imagine anybody would give you something for nothing?"

"Won't you take two dollars for it?" demanded Jim. "After we've done all this work?"

"I'm sorry," said the farmer. "This is the tree I ear-marked for my own wood. I sent this lad down right after lunch to cut it down and get the top cleared."

"Well," said the hired man. "I done it."

The Hard Way

Jim eased himself down in the water. I held up my pole and he gave two or three rapid kicks and splashes.

"I've decided," said Jim Frise, "not to go with you on your Quebec trip."

"Aw," said I.

"Those birch bark canoes you tell about," went on Jim; "I don't like the idea of fishing from a bark canoe."

"They're as steady as any other canoe," I protested.

"Sure," said Jim. "Since no canoe is steady."

"Well, you can swim, can't you?" I exclaimed. "This was to have been a good trip."

"No, I can't swim," stated Jim coolly.

"Can't swim!" I cried. "Can't swim! Good heavens, man, every Canadian ought to know how to swim almost as soon as he knows how to walk. Don't you know that one-half the area of Ontario is water?"

"Is it?" asked Jim.

"Take a look at any map," I went on. "Especially in the newer parts of the province. The map is half blue. I tell you your life is not safe in Ontario unless you can swim."

"I've got along all right so far," said Jim. "I've never even been dumped out of a canoe. Let's put it this way: Every Canadian ought to know how to swim or else he ought to keep out of boats. I keep out of boats, especially birch bark canoes."

"Swimming is as easy and natural," I said, "as walking. How is it you never learned to swim?"

"I don't know," said Jim. "I guess I just never had the opportunity to learn."

"Well, it's never too late," I said. "Swimming comes as natural to a man as it does to a duck. If I could teach you how to swim in the next few weeks would you come to Quebec with me?"

"How would you teach me?" asked Jim.

"Well, the best way is simply to throw a man in and he'll swim. But the most humane way is to get a long pole, like a clothesline prop, and tie a six-foot length of clothesline on it. Then you tie a belt around the pupil, tie a rope to the belt, have him get in the water and then with the teacher on the bank or wharf the swimmer strokes along, with the pole holding him up, and as he goes through the motions of swimming the first thing you know he is swimming, and the teacher quietly relaxes the support of the rope and pole. Presto! The pupil is swimming. That pole is just moral support. It gives confidence and gets the pupil over that feeling of doubt that, by motion of his arms and legs, he can keep himself on the surface."

"It sounds simple," said Jim.

"Listen, as soon as the Humber gets warm," I said, "let's go out and find a quiet swimming hole and I'll teach you, and then will you go to Quebec with me?"

"If I learn to swim," said Jim, "so that I feel confident I could look after myself in a bark canoe I'll go with you."

"Sold!" I shouted.

The last warm spell I got a clothes prop from my house and tied a stout piece of clothesline to it and stood it ready in the garage. Jimmie had got to the place in his cartoon where he has to write the words in the balloons, as they call them in the art circles, and I knew he always liked to run away from that. He hates spelling. So I walked over to him, staring at those empty spaces in Birdseye Center, and suggested that we take our first swimming lesson. At such a time Jim would accept almost any suggestion.

"Great!" he said. So we drove out and got our swimming suits and the long pole with rope.

"Where will we change into our swimming suits?" asked Jim.

"In the bushes," said I. "Let's be old-fashioned."

We drove out to the Humber and upstream a few miles looking for a good deep hole where Jim's long legs wouldn't touch bottom.

"I'm a little nervous," confessed Jim. "I've started to learn to swim a dozen times in my life, but I always lost my nerve at the last minute. It's funny how a thing like that gets into your very bones, isn't it? I just feel I'll never learn to swim."

"Listen," I assured him, "I'll have you swimming inside an hour."

"It sure will make me feel good," admitted Jim. "Whenever I'm fishing I always have that fear lurking in my mind."

"Boy," I cried, "to be able to sit in a canoe, even a

218

birch bark canoe, without any sense of fear is one of the most lovely sensations in the world. Fearless! It's a great way to be."

We came to a nice broad place in the river, and except for a few cows in the pasture beside the stream the place was deserted.

We parked the car and got into some bushes and changed into our swim suits. Jim's was one of those limp kind that dangled off him, while mine was just the least bit shrunk to my form. I got the long pole, an old belt, and we strolled down to the water.

"I feel pretty funny," said Jim, his arms wrapped around himself.

"Stage fright," I said.

"The water looks cold," said Jim, "and muddy."

"I thought you were a country fellow," I sneered.

"Suppose I practise the motions today," said Jim, "and then the next day I'll have the rope tied to me?"

"Suppose my neck," I said. "The way to learn to swim is just to jump in. The perfect way is to be pushed in and have to swim. I'm going to all this trouble with pole and rope just to make it easy for you. For Pete's sake!"

"All right," said Jimmie, submitting to the belt being strapped around him. We were down on the bank of the pool and I fastened the rope into the belt.

"Make it good and tight," said Jim. "Water makes knots slippery."

"Listen, I've taught scores."

"Come In and Save Me"

I could feel Jim shivering, although the day was perfect and the water almost lukewarm.

"Now," said I, "wade in."

"You go in first and give me a few lessons by demonstration," said Jim.

"And then stand out here and shiver while holding you on a pole?" I cried. "Go ahead; I've got you."

Jim put one toe in the water and snatched it out.

"Gee," he said, "I hate this."

"What's the matter?" I cried. "Haven't I got you on a rope big enough to hold a steamboat?"

Greg Clark & Jimmie Frise Outdoors

Jim stood with his arms around himself, staring at the water, and then, slowly, like a man in a trance, he stepped in and with a kind of pallid determination he waded in to his waist. He looked back at me with imploring eyes.

"Don't let go that pole," he chattered.

"Duck," I commanded.

Jim ducked.

"Now," I began, "lie forward in the water and take slow and easy strokes with your arms and kick out with your legs."

Jim squatted a couple of times and stood up.

"Are you holding me?" he quavered.

I hoisted the pole and Jim could feel the rope and belt tighten on him.

"All right, go ahead," I commanded.

Jim eased himself down in the water. I held up on the pole and he gave two or three rapid kicks and splashes, and stood up again, gasping and coughing.

"How's that?" he exclaimed proudly.

"Wait till we get you over here in the deeper water," I said.

I walked along the bank and towed Jim along.

"Now swim," I ordered.

Slowly Jim lifted one foot and then the other off the bottom and started to make excited and frantic motions with his arms and legs. Puffing and spluttering and splashing.

I pulled along the bank to get him into the deepest part of the hole.

Now nobody is sorrier than I am for what happened. In theory, the idea is to get your pupil in deep so that he has to trust the pole. Then, when he is actually swimming, ease off the pole and he sees he is swimming unaided.

In pulling Jim along I put too much strain on the knot which tied the rope to the pole. It simply slipped off the end, and there, to my horror, was Jim vanishing in the muddy pool.

"Jim," I screamed.

I did a very foolish thing. I threw the pole in to him.

His head popped up and he thrashed out and got hold of the pole. But it was too light to support him. He sank again, the pole slowly sticking upright out of the water as Jim clamped himself around it.

"Jimmie," I screamed again.

As if in reply, his head rose out of the water again and, spouting a mouthful of water, he croaked at me: "Come in and save me!"

"I can't swim," I confessed wildly.

Only a Theorist

Jim sank sadly out of sight again, the pole waving drunkenly out of the pool.

I was dancing along the bank, shouting, when I saw the pole go rigid, and I knew that Jim had stuck the lower end of it into the mud bottom of the swimming hole. To my joy, I saw Jim slowly emerge again, clinging to the pole like a monkey on a stick. He hung tenderly to it as it swayed, barely holding.

"Did you say you can't swim?" croaked Jim, spouting more water.

"Not a stroke," I said brokenly. "Jim, I'm so sorry! Wait until I get help."

"No," said Jim, coughing. "I'm going to learn to swim right now. You stay there and watch me."

His eyes glared with a mountainous effort of will. He took a deep breath. And then he let go the pole and, with strong, wide strokes, he fairly lifted himself through the water and grabbed the bank. Along the bank he pulled himself and I was there at the beach to hold out rescuing arms to him. I dragged him on to the beach, where he sagged exhausted. He clung to me desperately.

"Jimmie," I exulted, "you can swim!"

Jim rose to his feet, holding desperately to my arm.

"The best way to learn," he said, looking at me out of bloodshot eyes which glittered, "is just to be thrown in."

"That's what the best teachers say," I admitted a little nervously.

"To think of you," said Jim, "my dear friend, risking your life in birch bark canoes in Quebec, away off there, and not being able to swim."

"I'll learn, some day." I said brightly, "sooner or later."

"Sooner," said Jim.

He whirled me around. He took me by both elbows from behind, he hoisted me six feet in the air and threw me, in cold blood, right out into the middle of that deep, terrible pool.

I don't recall much. I came up once and saw Jimmie in the act of sitting down on the bank.

I came up twice, and saw Jim resting his chin on his elbows, watching me. I let out a yell, but the water got in.

I saw my past life passing before me. Not all my life, mostly the last few minutes. I wished I had told Jimmie I was only a theorist. But I felt sad for myself, because, after all, most of us are theorists anyway. We know a lot of things, but we don't have to be able to do them ourselves in order to tell others, do we? Politics, for example. Or how to run the war.

No Time Like the Present

I was just thinking about the war when I felt myself seized from behind in a terrific vise-like grip. I was hauled to the surface, and I took a vast breath of air when suddenly I felt a terrific blow on the chin. I went away, away.

The next thing I knew I was lying on the hard beach and Jim was jouncing me up and down around the stomach.

"Ah, back again?" he asked, turning my face up.

"Ooooooooh," I said.

"Sorry to have to sock you on the jaw," said Jim. "But the great danger in saving a drowning man is that he is likely to struggle and drown you, too. So the best thing to do is to sock him on the jaw, knock him out, then you can save him in peace."

"I see," I said weakly.

"As soon as you feel well enough," said Jim, "I'll teach you how to swim."

"Not today!" I cried.

"No time like the present."

"Jimmie, in my weakened condition, you wouldn't throw me in again?"

"It's the best way," said Jim. "Get it over with. After this experience you are likely to be so afraid you will never learn. I don't want you sitting all cringed up with fright in that birch bark canoe in Quebec."

"I feel faint," said I.

"Water will revive you," said Jim.

"If I wade in myself," I said, "and swim across that pool, will that be enough?"

Jim considered carefully.

"All right," he said.

"Get that pole in case I get into difficulty," I begged.

Jim took the pole and tied the rope back on it.

"The knot may hold," he said.

He stood by while I waded into the pool.

I lay forward and with great splashes and coughing swam across the pool. But what Jimmie does not know is that I had my feet on the bottom all the way across. At the far side I turned and swam back, then turned and swam grandly—but cautiously—out toward the middle of the pool where Jimmie had so nearly drowned and touched bottom all the way.

There wasn't a foot of the pond over my head. If Jim had not had his knees bent up in horror, as he plunged and splashed, he would not have been in over his armpits.

"Good boy," said Jim, admiringly, as I stroked grandly around the pool.

When I got tired I crawled ashore and Jim assisted me.

"Good for you," he shouted. "Isn't it great to know how to swim?"

So we dried and dressed, like old friends again, and drove back to town.

And it is nice to know not only that I am a good teacher, but, what is more to the point, that from now on one of us can swim.